Dominion and Liberty

Arthur S. Link
General Editor for History

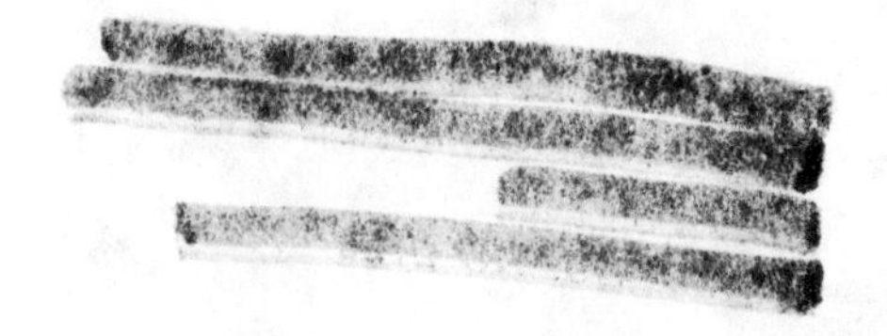

Dominion and Liberty

IDEOLOGY IN THE ANGLO-AMERICAN WORLD 1660–1801

Robert M. Calhoon
The University of North Carolina
at Greensboro

HARLAN DAVIDSON, INC.
ARLINGTON HEIGHTS, ILLINOIS 60004

Library of Congress Cataloging-in-Publication Data

Calhoon, Robert M. (Robert McCluer)
Dominion and liberty: ideology and the Anglo-American world, 1660–1801/Robert M. Calhoon.
p. cm.
Includes bibliographical references and index.
ISBN 0-88295-913-1
1. Political science—Great Britain—History—17th century.
2. Political science—Great Britain—History—18th century.
3. Great Britain—Politics and government—1660–1714.
4. Great Britain—Politics and government—18th century.
5. Political science—United States—History—17th century. 6. Political science—United States—History—18th century. 7. United States—Politics and government—Revolution, 1775–1783. 8. United States—Politics and government—1783–1809. I. Title.
JA84.G4C35 1994
320'.0941—dc20 93-21383
CIP

Cover illustration: (See p. 58.) Courtesy Library of Congress.

Manufactured in the United States of America
98 97 96 95 94 1 2 3 4 5 MG

In Memory
of Carol Robbins
and Jane Stump

Contents

Acknowledgments

Arthur S. Link and Cheryl F. Junk read successive drafts of this book and filled the margins of the manuscript with questions, suggestions, and comments that vastly improved its clarity and coherence.

Over the years several students have discussed the subject of ideology of the American Revolution with me—so carefully that I cannot tell where their insights left off and mine began—especially Trudy Freesland Doster, Marsha Buckalew Driscoll, Shelley Bobb, David R. Turner, Thomas T. Taylor, Earl Fox, Kenneth Anthony, and Doug Bristol. I am also grateful to Scott Culclasure, Karen Raley, David Thornton, Charles Wheeler, Joshua McKaughan, Seth Hinshaw, Mary Ellis, Damon Hickey, John Riley, Frank Dale, Chris McKee, and Joseph Beasley.

Joyce Appleby, William Link, Converse Clowse, Bradley Macdonald, Stephen Ruzicka, Karl Schleunes, Paul Mazgaj, Frank Melton, Hugh Parker, Susan Shelmerdine, Clyde Ellis, James Evans, David Olson, Mary Helms, Mack Bulgin, and Robert Weir instructed me in matters beyond my competence. Henry Levinson and Walter Beale have made the College of Arts and Sciences at the University of North Carolina at Greensboro a good place to study and teach discourse. Sigrid Walker keeps me apprised of the publication and availability of scores of new books every year, and she deserves credit for whatever bibliographical thoroughness the book has.

Bernard Bailyn answered my questions about Thomas Hutchinson and John Dickinson. Peter Onuf read the manuscript for the publisher and prepared a rigorous, constructive critique. My interest in eighteenth-century politics and ideology began in England in 1962–64 under the direction of my teachers, Jack P. Greene and J. R. Pole—whose writings inform almost every page of this book—and with the help of my friends John Dunn and Gordon Schocket. Maureen G. Hewitt and Andrew J. Davidson edited the book with care and insight. Lori Watson prepared the index.

Mark Riegel and Todd Drake are loyal and understanding friends and along with Ellie Barrett, Y Thien Nie, Y Bham Nie, and Y Nuh Ecam have taught me a great deal about the meaning of liberty.

My wife Doris has been a constant source of encouragement, and our daughter, Claudia Marie, has urged me to heed the plaque on my office wall that reads "Eschew Obfuscation" when I write about ideas.

Robert M. Calhoon
Greensboro, North Carolina
April 1, 1993

John Dickinson, Letters of a Pennsylvania Farmer. *Courtesy of the John Carter Brown Library at Brown University.*

CHAPTER ONE

Ideology as a Way of Thinking about the American Revolution

LIKE all revolutions, the American Revolution was a complex, intriguing, controversial event—for those living through it and for those who ponder its history. And as with other revolutions, participation and historical scholarship both begin in specific human situations. This chapter will examine five situations that span the spectrum of insights into Revolutionary reality. The consideration of a *political* situation is followed by examples of *constitutional*, *economic*, and *social* realities, and, finally, by an example of the Revolution viewed as an *ideological* experience. Thus, this chapter will introduce the American Revolution and, more important, indicate the interlocking character of its different perspectives.

Political Conflict

On August 5, 1774, a crowd of more than one hundred Hampshire County, Massachusetts, men "in a tumultuous manner" surrounded William Williams, Israel Stoddard, and Woodbridge Little—three of the most prominent and respected figures in the county—and demanded answers to some pressing political questions. Why had they incited divisions among the people? Why had they opposed public denunciation of the Coercive Acts? Was it not true that "in general" they "were enemies to the Constitution of this province, Tories, &c.?" The leaders of the crowd demanded to know whether Williams, Stoddard, or Little had received political appointments from General Thomas Gage, who a month earlier had become Massachusetts royal governor. The three denied that they had. They were then asked to sign a statement confessing their complicity in the enforcement of the Coercive Acts. Asking what "alternative" they had, they were told that the surrounding crowd was growing impatient and might get out of hand. "We judged we had nothing to expect but severity and violence unless we somehow appeased them," Williams later explained. They spent the next two hours negotiating with their tormenters the terms of a new statement that reduced their "concessions" to "certain senseless and unnecessary propositions": that the recent acts of Parliament were unconstitutional (the trio took comfort in the fact that no law was specified and that, for all they knew, the hated Massachusetts Government Act had not yet received the royal assent), that the people were entitled to resent and oppose such laws, and that they would not "countenance" enforcement of such laws in Massachusetts nor "discountenance" resistance by "the people." After signing this pledge, the three men were allowed to depart.

This confrontation between prominent allies of the Crown in western Massachusetts and a Revolutionary crowd was a *political* event involving neighbors who knew each other well. Williams was forty years old when this episode occurred. His father was Israel Williams, the most powerful of the so-called "River Gods," powerful landowners and political magnates tied by friendship, marriage, and political association to Governor Thomas Hutchinson, Chief Justice Peter Oliver, and their kinsmen and allies in Boston who represented the interests of the British Crown in Massachusetts. William Williams was a respected and conscientious clerk of the Court of Common Pleas in Hampshire County. After his close brush with mob violence he conducted himself, according to his minister, with such "prudence, discretion, and evident integrity" that he stayed out of trouble, though he had to resign his lucrative office and retire to one of his father's farms in adjoining Berkshire County. Stoddard, seven years younger than Williams, had a rougher encounter with Revolutionary justice—though one which ended as happily. He fled to occupied New York City in 1776 but, rather than see his property confiscated, returned home in 1777 to confess his political misdeeds and plead for forgiveness. Falling under suspicion again, he was arrested and this time saved himself by taking an oath of allegiance to the United States. After that he lived peacefully in Pittsfield, Massachusetts, until his death in 1782. Woodbridge Little also survived his reputation as a Tory, and in 1782 he chaired a Berkshire County convention condemning the kind of agrarian disorders that three years later erupted as Shays's Rebellion.

The political struggle in which Williams, Stoddard, and Little became embroiled in 1774 marked the breakdown of a fragile stability in Massachusetts. Leaders of the province had long prided themselves on a political system that was an amalgam of popular democracy, aristocratic stability, and an energizing royal administration. Caught up in the economic growth of the Connecticut River valley, most residents of the region deferred to the "River Gods." But prosperity cut two ways, keeping men on the make too busy to engage in politics and also creating new towns in which people became less accustomed to, and dependent on, the leadership of the grandees of the older, inland towns. The news of the Coercive Acts electrified the residents of these younger, more self-conscious, western Massachusetts towns and suddenly made the sons of the River Gods vulnerable to insult and attack. The most controversial of the four Coercive Acts, the Massachusetts Government Act, had abolished the upper house of the Massachusetts colonial legislature, the members of which had been elected since 1692 by the lower house, and replaced it with an appointed Royal Council. Both Israel Williams and his kinsman, John Worthington, had been named to the new Council. By the time the two men faced an angry crowd on August 30, Israel had already renounced his seat but Worthington had not. One observer reported how

> the sight of him [Worthington] flashed lightening from their eyes. Their spirits were already raised and the sight of this object [i.e., the once proud Worthington] gave them additional force. He had not refused his new office of counsellor. For that reason he was very obnoxious. But the people kept their tempers. He attempted to harrangue them in mitigation of his conduct, but was soon obliged to desist. The people were not to be dallied with. Nothing would satisfy them but a renunciation.

The capitulation of all of the new Royal Councillors who faced popular crowds in the Massachusetts countryside in August and September 1774 convinced General Gage in Boston that he could not restore order in the province without a major show of military force. When that news reached London, the ministry concluded that Gage had lost his nerve and decided to remove him from command.

Constitutional Conflict

Massachusetts had reacted viscerally to the Coercive Acts because the abrogation of the colony's 1691 charter jeopardized political liberty in the province. A similar dispute in South Carolina, dating back to 1769, also threatened to annul a cardinal principle in that colony's political life and contributed to the collapse of British authority in 1775. On December 8, 1769, the Commons House of Assembly ordered the province's Treasurer to contribute £ 1,500 sterling of public funds to the Society of Gentlemen Supporters of the Bill of Rights in London—an aristocratic club raising funds to pay the debts of the British radical John Wilkes. South Carolina had been stung by criticism from Boston that it had failed to support the boycott against the Townshend duties earlier that year. Individuals in Boston and in Virginia had pledged gifts to Wilkes, but South Carolina's financial contribution was the only such support to come from a governmental body. This initiative placed the colony in the forefront of American supporters of the movement to democratize British political institutions. South Carolina's contribution to the Wilkes fund angered Colonial Secretary Lord Hillsborough, who instructed the acting governor, William Bull, to veto all appropriations bills until the House renounced its authority to send funds outside of the province without the governor's concurrence. Stymied by Bull's determination to veto money bills, the Assembly resorted to issuing informal IOUs to the province's creditors. Impasse set in. Perhaps unwittingly, the Crown had required that the South Carolina elite commit an act of self-abasement—unthinkable to these proud, sensitive men—as the price for restoring the normal fiscal operations of government. Therefore, the province's Commons House refused to become what one member called Hillsborough's "footstool." The ongoing dispute, from 1769 to 1775, created a poisonous atmosphere of distrust in South Carolina during the closing years of British rule.

The Wilkes fund controversy in South Carolina was a *constitutional* struggle. The Commons House, since 1691, had enjoyed the power to initiate legislation, and in 1756 the Council, or upper house, had conceded that the Commons House alone could enact appropriation bills. By custom and precedent, therefore, the Commons House possessed the power of the purse. Hillsborough's instruction to Bull, disciplining the House for its contribution to Wilkes's supporters, scuttled eight decades of precedent by asserting royal authority over fiscal decisions in Charleston. As the spokesman for the House declared, "the unconstitutional mandate of a minister" suddenly took precedence over "the ancient and undoubted" constitution of the province. The Crown's attempt to subvert historical constitutional practice taught Henry Laurens, a South Carolina merchant, that "the representative body of the people in [South] Carolina...have and ought to enjoy all the rights and privileges of a free people."

Constitutionalism was a familiar and vital body of ideas in the Anglo-American colonial world. Imperial officials and colonial leaders alike agreed that the victory of Parliament over the Crown in the Glorious Revolution of 1688–89 had inaugurated a new era in which constitutional principles—as set forth in historic documents—defined and limited the power of government. These leaders also usually agreed that the constitutional rights and privileges of British citizens were extended to the colonists—so far as was practicable. Determining what was practicable, however, created conflicts. But constitutionalism drove political conflict in the colonies for a more fundamental reason: during the seventeenth century, English constitutional theorists had split over an issue known as "prescription" vs. "custom." Prescription held that power was an intrinsic feature of the monarchy; custom held that practice and experience limited that intrinsic royal authority. The Glorious Revolution gave victory to the advocates of custom without entirely discrediting the claims of prescription. Thereafter, Parliament and the Crown papered over this theoretical disagreement by fusing the authority of Parliament and the Crown into a single kind of legitimate authority. As the imperial bureaucracy expanded in the eighteenth century, and searched for a theoretical basis for asserting wider control over the colonies, the theory of prescription crept back into use. Recognizing what was happening, colonial legislative spokesmen appealed again to custom as the bulwark of liberty. Although the prescription-custom struggle had an unexpected conclusion (see pp. 54–56 below), this kind of constitutionalism energized colonial politics during the pre-Revolutionary decade.

Economic Conflict

Explosive political conditions and destabilizing changes in constitutional practice may not, in and of themselves, have been sufficient to trigger a revolution. But once combined with fissures deep in the mercantilist structure of the British Empire, a more ominous picture began to emerge. The East India Company was one such fissure. A government-created monopoly conducting, since 1709, all British trade with India, the company had come by the 1770s to resemble the state monopolies in the Soviet Union before *perestroika*—uncompetitive, inefficient, bloated bureaucracies hobbled with debt and driven to adopt one short-term expedient after another. A suspicious ministry under British Treasurer Lord North stripped the company of much of its autonomy, but this commendable effort to discipline the aging giant of British mercantilism was undercut by the government's own hankering for a painless solution to the problem of its American colonies. When Chancellor of the Exchequer Charles Townshend prevailed on Parliament to tax lead, paint, glass, paper, and tea exports to America in 1767—what became known as the infamous Townshend duties—he also negotiated a five-year deal with the East India Company that rebated a 1745 tax on tea exports to America and Ireland; in return the company promised to reimburse the British Treasury for any revenue shortfall resulting from this arrangement. This expedient benefitted neither the company nor the government, and by the early 1770s the company was in even deeper financial trouble. Hoping to profit from increased tea sales in the home market, the company kept its domestic prices high. Sales languished, and the company then yearned to export duty-free tea to the European continent as yet another quick fix.

North balked. He offered instead a system by which bulk exports of tea would go directly to designated consignees in America. By eliminating the usual competitive auctions, the price of tea would become almost low enough to undersell the Dutch smugglers. However, North insisted on retaining the old Townshend duty on tea. The company opposed this step, and no one in Parliament spoke in its favor (the old tea duty did not even contribute to government revenue because it went into a special fund to pay the salaries of embattled Crown officials). North had insisted on the tea duty as a direct rebuke to ungrateful American colonists—"I know the temper of the people," he explained archly. "A stubborn Lord North," historian Benjamin W. Labaree observed in 1964, "had unwittingly hammered a nail into the coffin of the old British Empire."

What North could not comprehend was that his stick-and-carrot approach toward the East India Company—disciplining first and then providing a regulatory means for it to regain profitability—would exacerbate another *economic* difficulty in the empire. A severe credit crisis struck the empire in late 1772 and early 1773—coinciding with the drafting of the Tea Act. In response to the credit crunch, Massachusetts enacted a law severely curtailing licenses for auctioneers of imported goods. Merchants ruined by their sudden exclusion from export trade and tea merchants who were not lucky enough to have been designated as consignees thus composed a large audience that was ready to believe reports which one historian has characterized as "a vast conspiratorial plan to subvert American commerce." These stunned and angry merchants were almost certainly members of the crowd that boarded the first ship bearing tea shipped under the Tea Act, on December 16, 1773, and threw its cargo into Boston Harbor in the Boston Tea Party.

Social Stress

Historians have analyzed this mixture of political, constitutional, and economic disturbance in at least two ways. One approach has detected pervasive *social* stress in colonial society, particularly in what was seemingly the most stable and successful colony, Virginia. Though deeply in debt to British merchants and living beyond its means, the Virginia plantation gentry was a public-spirited, conscientious aristocracy. They lived integrated, dutiful, rewarding lives tending their plantations, managing the export of their tobacco crop, supervising their slaves, marrying off their children advantageously, operating local government as justices of the peace, and, for the most politically experienced, serving in the House of Burgesses. Theirs was a way of life demanding hard work, knowledge of public affairs, the cultivation of good relationships with kinsmen and contemporaries, and financial acumen. They viewed their fellow planter, George Mason, as the ideal embodiment of their collective values and abilities; "second to none in wisdom and virtue," and "of the first order of wisdom among those who acted on the theater of the Revolution, of expansive mind, profound judgment, cogent in argument, learned in the lore of former constitutions." Mason chose the Roman republican patriot, Cicero, as the model for his oratory and the Roman republican martyr, Cato, as the exemplar of a public man bound by conscience. He actually disliked the political life he practiced so skillfully, preferring always the privacy of his estate and library. The Virginia gentry saw in this kind of patriotism and duty a way to survive the political storms aroused by parliamentary taxation.

The pre-Revolutionary controversy, however, coincided with a severe crisis of confidence among the Virginia planters. Financially overextended, they had trouble earning enough sterling to remain solvent. Then in 1766, the death of the colony's Treasurer and Speaker of the House of Burgesses, John Robinson, revealed a massive embezzlement of public funds, which Robinson had used to help financially distressed friends and associates. That same year, an enraged but sober planter, John Chiswell, murdered a drunken merchant, Robert Routledge, in what one contemporary called "a strong fit of aristocratic insolence." Both the Robinson scandal and the Routledge murder called into question the competence and public spiritedness of Virginia's leadership.

Throughout the 1750s and 1760s, slaveowners in the Old Dominion began to worry about the brutality of their labor system—and their own safety. As a remedy, some planters promoted able slaves to skilled positions and even, in some cases, to managerial posts. The opportunity to talk to these slaves about plantation matters—and to reward these "acculturated" slaves with better living conditions—seemed to make slavery a less dangerous system for whites to maintain. Others knew better; Mason called slavery "a slow poison which is daily contaminating the minds and morals of our people," and most acts of resistance or subversion by slaves involved these seemingly acculturated or privileged slaves. The very prosperity that slavery undergirded had, by the 1730s and 1740s, raised Virginia's poor whites upward to the level of yeomen farmers, but by the 1750s and 1760s the spread of Baptist revivalism gave many of these still hard-pressed farmers a strong group identity and a moral aversion to the ostentatious lifestyle of the planters.

All of these kinds of social stress kept Virginia's leadership on edge during the late 1760s and early 1770s. Virginia's emphatic embrace of the cause of liberty in 1774–75 reflected apprehension as well as hope. Fear of social disorder at first made the gentry cautious about attacks against imperial authority, but once convinced that British policies jeopardized control of their own affairs and might even spawn disorder within the colony, the gentry moved swiftly, gracefully, and with near unanimity to construct a moral definition of their own society and values as a bulwark against the tyrannical designs of the British.

Ideology

The other way historians have chosen to interrelate the political, constitutional, and economic ingredients in the Revolution—and also to account for evidence of social stress—has been to identify the ideology that its leaders and participants shared. The term "ideology" itself has a curious history during the twentieth-century. From the 1920s to the 1940s, it signified the mindset of extremists so scarred by moral outrage that they embraced a rigid and intolerant social and political morality. Since the late 1950s, political scientists, and then many historians, have adopted a more generous view of ideology as a structure of perceptions, convictions, and diagnoses that are compelling enough to exert explanatory force over current events and thrust people into political action. By entering into the cluster of assumptions, ideas, beliefs, values, and moral and social imperatives of the Revolutionary generation, students of ideology attempt to look out at the world through the eyes of the Revolutionaries and see political reality as they saw it.

Bernard Bailyn's *The Ideological Origins of the American Revolution* (1967) almost single-handedly persuaded students of the Revolution to understand the event in these terms. That book, it should be noted, reproduced Bailyn's 1965 essay, "The Transforming Radicalism of the American Revolution," which was the "General Introduction" to Volume I of his edition of *The Pamphlets of the American Revolution*. That volume contained fourteen primary pamphlets, each with an introduction by Bailyn. His introduction to the Stamp Act pamphlet by John Dickinson provides exceptional insight into the personal and social meaning of Revolutionary ideology.

Dickinson was not a likely figure to become a Revolutionary ideologue. The son of a wealthy Maryland landowner and lawyer, he studied at the Inns of Court in London in the mid-1750s. English legal and political institutions thrilled him as much as the corruption and squalor of London appalled him. After establishing himself as a lawyer in Philadelphia in 1757, he entered politics as a member of the Quaker party, and in 1770 he married into a powerful Quaker family. Though an Anglican, he imbibed Quaker peaceableness and distaste for conflict as well as the aristocratic assurance of the Quaker grandees. His love of the law was more scholarly and humanistic than professional and legalistic. Thus he was more at home in his study than in the courtroom or the hurly-burly of politics. *"And yet for all of this*—[Bailyn argues] *for all his wealth, position, occupational bias, moral sensibility, and temperamental constraint—Dickinson was a radical: a radical in the vital sense in which the Revolution itself was radical"* (italics added).

In this context, "radical" means literally the root of the matter. Dickinson's political writings in the 1760s and 1770s went to the heart of the controversy between Britain and the colonies in two ways. First, he had read, internalized, and embraced a large body of English libertarian writings known as the country ideology, which conceived of all political life—indeed all of social existence—as a struggle between liberty and oppression. Oppression was closely linked to conspiracy and corruption, liberty to virtue and republicanism. Power in this system was ravenous and constantly expanding; freedom was fragile and always vulnerable. Only conscience and civic duty upheld liberty while self-interest and egotism energized the forces of dominion. Based on Renaissance and Roman republican writings and elaborated in brilliant British criticisms of ministers such as Sir Robert Walpole, the country ideology was subtle, elegant, and captivating. Dickinson employed it brilliantly.

Secondly, Dickinson's application of these ideas to pre-Revolutionary politics was even more radical. His *Letters of a Pennsylvania Farmer* (1768) was the first writing by an American to detect a pattern in such diverse British measures as expanded vice-admiralty jurisdiction, the Stamp Act, the Townshend duties, and the presence of the British army in America in times of peace. For Dickinson, these were not just the isolated actions of heavy-handed British legislation and administration; they indicated "an inveterate resolution...to annihilate the liberties" of the colonists. The only effective opposition to ministerial conspiracy was a trade boycott backed up by ideological, political, material, and religious solidarity: "Let us invent, let us work, let us save, let us at the same time keep up our claims and unceasingly repeat our complaints.... Above all, let us implore the protection of that infinite good and gracious Being by whom kings reign and princes decree justice." At a dinner in 1769, 350 Boston activists joined in singing the chorus to the "Liberty Song," based on Dickinson's pamphlet, in what John Adams called "cultivating the sensations of freedom."

Ideology and the Sociology of Knowledge

The five foregoing sketches are not microcosms of the Revolution, though they are complementary parts of a larger whole. The first three, centering on politics, constitutionalism, and economics, are drawn from historical events, while those on social stress and ideology reflect perspectives that were constructed recently by historians. To these could be added cultural, military, and even psychological manifestations as well. Therefore, though the Revolution remains one event, its manifestations are interrelated parts of a larger whole. For example, the political crisis in western Massachusetts towns became an economic issue when newer and more rapidly growing towns undercut the older, established centers of trade and government. Moreover, hostility toward the "River Gods" and their families was ideological as much as it was merely political; the destruction of the elected Council was a constitutional crisis. In the case of the social stresses felt by the Virginia elite, symptoms of that malaise were economic difficulties; yet the social stress experienced by the gentry provoked some of the most elegant statements of constitutionalism and ideology in Revolutionary America. The same variety of motives, problems, and processes can be found in the Wilkes fund crisis in South Carolina, in the economics that led to the tea crisis, and in the impact of Dickinson's *Letters of a Pennsylvania Farmer*. The purpose of categorizing historical insights as political, constitutional, economic, social, or constitutional is to cast a focused beam of light on the institutions, individuals, written pronouncements, and critical events that compose a revolution in human affairs.

Troublesome questions nonetheless haunt an ideological interpretation of the Revolution: Did the Revolutionary struggle pit a patriot ideology of liberty against a rival British, or loyalist, ideology of obedience and order? Within the American Revolutionary imagination, was the republicanism of the country ideology the dominant philosophy, or did it share common ground with a Lockean ideology of consent and with other systems of political insight? What does ideology measure? Reality? Danger? Possibility?

Americans had hoped that George III would turn out to be a "patriot king" true to the best traditions of British liberty, but they concluded reluctantly that the king and his court were "wretched, covetous, and tyrannical" and surely implicated in the usurpation of colonial liberties. Appeal to a patriot king enabled the people to remain free through timely action, but the recognition that monarchies were incapable of wisdom and benevolence indicated that their doom was sealed. Therefore, did a two-faced ideology lead the people onward in purposeful action, or did it merely warn them that the way ahead was strewn with danger?

The jury is still out on these questions. Whether an ideology of hierarchy and order confronted republican ideology, or whether the mother country and her loyalist champions were too fixated on questions of power and national interest to actually appreciate the values and morality of an ideological view, is not yet known. Whether Lockean ideology offered an alternative to republicanism, or simply conceded the Revolutionary high ground to an ideology of republican virtue, is not a question historians can with unanimity answer. And whether their historical knowledge and insight allowed the patriots to make reasonable choices or simply defined for them the stark choice between acting upon an heroic virtue or accepting an abject submission is a question that probes the deepest levels of our assumptions about politics, society, and human nature.

Historians have, at the same time, sharpened the way they ask these questions. How then do historians move from asking better questions to shaping answers into new interpretations? For nearly a century, colonial historians have realized that the restoration of Charles II in 1660, and even more important the Glorious Revolution of 1688, released powerful organizing energies into the English-speaking world. Some argue—as some colonists did—that the English Civil War of the 1640s, and even the Norman Conquest of 1066, shaped American political development. But 1660 marks the beginning of a coherent, ongoing story of English dominion and the American colonial response to that dominion.

The institutional, or imperial, historians of the Revolution, writing at the turn of this century, had a deep admiration for British imperialism and regretted the shortsightedness of the rebellious colonists of the 1770s. The progressive historians of the early decades of the twentieth century identified rival social classes in colonial America: an aristocracy and a merchant class that both benefitted from British rule, a common class that was exploited by it, and a segment of the elite who actually had more to gain from political independence than from the perpetuation of British rule. Neither the imperial nor the progressive school needed a concept of ideology. Economic self-interest, class consciousness, and the notion that propaganda was a deliberate, cynical, political tool answered most of their questions about political thought.

This insensitivity to the consideration of people's motivations gave way after World War II as a new generation of early American historians, called "neo-whigs," replaced the imperial and progressive schools. Like nineteenth-century whig historians, the neo-whigs saw liberty as the core of the Revolution, and they took the words of colonial protest seriously. Unlike the older historians, the neo-whigs were careful not to wax moralistic or nationalistic, and they appreciated the complexity and irony of politics. The neo-whigs fell under the influence of a development known as "center-periphery" sociology. According to this view, the British Empire contained a powerful *center* in southern England that was enriched as well as troubled by the resource-rich developing territories on the *periphery* of the English metropolitan world. (Historians using this framework include Ireland, Wales, Scotland, the colonies, and trading bases in Africa and India on the periphery). People at the center are considered to be less prone to ideological thinking, while those on the periphery have a much greater propensity to see political and economic issues in moral terms. Those at the center live close to the institutions that parcel out power and advantage, while those on the periphery feel far less secure about shifts in power and policy and depend more on ideas and moral instincts to gain political leverage.

The center/periphery model continues to dominate colonial and Revolutionary historical scholarship, but with an important new qualification. The collapse of communism in the former Soviet Union and eastern Europe—ostensibly a prime example of center/periphery conflict—cautions against the casual assumptions that centers necessarily become overbearing, making peripheries the seedbeds of liberty. Sometimes it is the peripheral regions that contain and nourish violent, reactionary, and despotic habits that are only held in check by imperial rule. Edmund Burke appreciated this characteristic in rebellious, subordinate communities when he warned Parliament, in 1775, that precisely because patriot leaders in the southern colonies were slaveowners, they would fight for liberty with fierce, almost fanatical, zeal.

Even before center/periphery sociology reoriented the study of the British Empire, a related intellectual development—the publication of Karl Mannheim's *Ideology and Utopia* in 1936—awakened curiosity among historians about the purposes of political discourse. Mannheim was a refugee from Nazi Germany who joined the faculty of the London School of Economics in 1933. He proposed subjecting "the total structure of consciousness and thought" of political leaders and movements to "thoroughgoing sociological analysis." Going beyond criticism—beyond showing that a political idea or goal was wrong or misguided or deceitful—Mannheim believed that sociology could comprehend the interaction of all the cultural debts, human desires, and shared values that permeate politics and society. He called this vision "the sociology of knowledge."

During the post–World War II period, Mannheim came to exert a profound influence on political and intellectual historians. A book that expressed well the utility of his ideas was *Ideology and Discontent* (1961) edited by David Apter. Apter emphasized the "mirror-like quality" of ideology "reflecting the same moral and material aspects of our understanding" that Mannheim had included in the sociology of knowledge. The most influential paper in Apter's book was an essay by the cultural anthropologist Clifford Geertz, "Ideology as a Cultural System." In elegant conceptualization and language, Geertz juxtaposed science and ideology as the dual tendencies of human consciousness in the modern world. "Where science is the diagnostic, the critical, dimension of culture, ideology is the justificatory, the apologetic one.... Science names the structures of situations..., [and] its style is restrained, spare, and analytical.... By objectifying moral sentiment, ideology...seeks to motivate action.... Its style is ornate, vivid, deliberately subjective." History, including the history of revolutions, involves both these kinds of consciousness; Geertz's achievement was to persuade historians that both facts and values need to be discovered by immersion in sources from the past and that the history of ideology deserves to be written in a style that expresses its subjectivity and moral seriousness.

Quite independently of this new interest in political language, Caroline Robbins published in 1961 the fruits of a quarter century of research on British libertarian thought, *The Eighteenth-Century Commonwealthman*, which brought to light for the first time ideas about liberty and justice voiced by religious dissenters, English political radicals, and Scottish and Irish intellectuals that had rippled through British and colonial politics and society.

Then in 1964, J. G. A. Pocock, a historian of political thought teaching in New Zealand, brought Geertz's concept of ideology and Robbins's evidence of British libertarianism together in a paper entitled "Machiavelli, Harrington, and English Political Ideologues in the Eighteenth Century." Focussing on the most important of Robbins's commonwealthmen, the country party critics of Sir Robert Walpole, Pocock argued that these writers diagnosed dangerous moral and political flaws in British society. Circulated in manuscript before it was published in 1965, this essay influenced Bailyn. Pocock and Robbins moved Bailyn beyond his neo-whig view that "the American Revolution was above all else an ideological-constitutional struggle and not primarily a controversy between social groups undertaken to force changes in the organization of society," to see the Revolution as "a radical idealization and rationalization of the previous century and a half of American experience."

Bailyn incorporated Pocock's conception of ideology as morally diagnostic into his introduction to *The Pamphlets of the American Revolution* because he found that the American patriots had an insatiable appetite for moral criticism with which to defend themselves against British imperial presumption and arrogance.

Conclusion: The Structure of an Ideological Interpretation

In just over four years (1961–1965) Robbins, Geertz, Pocock, and Bailyn detonated a scholarly avalanche that has not yet ceased moving masses of evidence and reinterpretation before students of eighteenth-century history. Avalanches defy precise description, but three characteristics of this one can be identified. The ideological history of the Anglo-American world, in the first place, existed in the larger context of what Robert R. Palmer called *The Age of the Democratic Revolution* in a two-volume work published in 1959 and 1964. Palmer argues that the American and French revolutions occurred during an era of social and political unrest throughout Europe and North America that included significant ferment in Great Britain, Ireland, Poland, the Low Countries, and the Hapsburg Empire. In a chapter entitled "Aristocracy about 1760: Theory and Practice," Palmer suggested that throughout Europe the ruling class sensed that profound social change was imminent and that many had anticipated it with apprehensive excitement. While each locality in the Atlantic world had its own peculiar needs and potentialities, Palmer taught students of the eighteenth century, on the eve of the ideological interpretation, to remember the international scope of revolutionary change.

A second essential feature of recent historiography of the American and French revolutions is an appreciation of the new rhetoric of politics in the late eighteenth century. Breaking with the ornate language and complex presentation of Augustan oratory and literature, the new rhetoricians in Britain rejected, in the words of one contemporary, "all the amplifications, digressions, and swellings of style" of high culture "to return back the primitive purity, and shortness, when men delivered [important ideas] almost in an equal number of words." This new rhetoric stressed concrete facts, images, simplicity, and directness as the key to human communication.

Third, the new ideological history put down roots into the conceptual soil of "political culture" as a way of viewing politics. The term "political culture" was coined by students of comparative political systems in the early 1960s, at about the same time that ideology became a focus of scholarly activity. It refers to the unwritten rules of politics that everyone within any culture implicitly understands and accepts. In stable political times, political culture reflects the values and aspirations of the age; in a revolutionary period, a new political culture of change validates and informs the principles and actions of reformers and radicals alike.

During the 1960s, the Civil Rights movement and protests against the Vietnam War changed the whole climate of politics in the United States by injecting new standards of morality into public life and polarizing public discussion. Then during the 1970s and 1980s, the feminist movement, the antiabortion cause, and gay liberation ignited cultural conflicts that remain unresolved. Each of these movements demanded, and in some cases achieved, political and legal changes that have become part of the fabric of American society. At the same time, each has generated powerful ideas, apprehensions, and expectations that have become a new rhetoric of protest in the political culture of the United States during the late twentieth century.

Portrait of the Reverend Samuel Johnson by John Smibert. *Columbia University in the City of New York.*

CHAPTER TWO

The English Philosophy of Order, 1660–1714

BEFORE there was an American ideology of liberty, there was an English philosophy of order. During Elizabeth's reign, Shakespeare had glorified the stabilizing, civilizing work of strong monarchy and condemned the violent, conspiratorial, restless habits of aristocratic opposition to the Crown. The philosophy of order was not a stagnant orthodoxy. Reverence for order coexisted with other English political habits and intellectual achievements. In *Order, Empiricism, and Politics: Two Traditions of English Political Thought, 1500–1700* (1964), W. H. Greenleaf has placed that philosophy in a larger context. By comparing the philosophy of order with the rise of scientific inquiry (empiricism), Greenleaf locates the origins of the constitutional doctrines of "prescription" and "custom," discussed in Chapter One. The seventeenth-century idea that the well-being of a nation depended on the continuity of royal authority—and the continuity of other historic institutions like the established church and the landed aristocracy—was not a royalist fabrication. A long tradition stretching back to medieval theorists, revitalized in the late eighteenth century by Edmund Burke, vindicated prescribed order as the bedrock of the English, and later, the British nation.

Challenging, but also infiltrating and strengthening that philosophy of order between 1500 and 1700, was an appreciation of empiricism, which made sensory experiences and the scientific collection of data the proper basis for evaluating political institutions and determining the limits of their authority. Empiricism appeared to have displaced order as the core of public philosophy in late–seventeenth-century England. But in actuality, empiricists also sought to preserve tradition, by discerning its historical basis, and to protect constituted authority by rationally justifying its legitimacy. Empiricism became the basis of the Enlightenment of the eighteenth century, but during that period the institutions of church and state, often invigorated by the new rationalism, perpetuated the existing political and social order.

Between the Restoration of Charles II in 1660 and the accession of George I in 1714, England achieved political stability by resolving the inherent tension between the power of the king and the authority of Parliament (in favor of Parliament) and by securing the Protestant succession to the throne. The struggle for parliamentary supremacy and Protestant succession taught English men and women that ambitious Stuart monarchs, backed by absolutist Catholic France, engendered fear and apprehension in the land, and that the international forces of Protestantism and the new ideas about the constitutional limitation of royal authority could be mobilized by Parliament and the people. Neither the philosophy of order nor the emergent spirit of empiricism were full-blown ideologies. The links between thought and action were not as tightly drawn in the seventeenth century as they would become in the next century. And during this pre-Enlightenment era, the self-conscious discussion of power had not yet become as widespread as it would be in the eighteenth century. However, the English concept of order in the late seventeenth and early eighteenth centuries was surely the beginning of an ideology that would come into its own during the Augustan era, from 1714 to the 1750s, when British power and wealth resembled that of first-century Rome during the reign of Caesar Augustus.

Like the later ideologies of the eighteenth century—the country ideology, American republicanism, and even French revolutionary radicalism—English ideas about order and empiricism crossed the Atlantic and there evoked responses that reverberated back to Europe. This chapter will examine that trans-Atlantic crisscrossing of ideas through the Anglo-American world from 1660 to 1714.

Proprietary Colonization

The restoration monarchy of Charles II (1660–1685) was the source of the most concentrated dose of order ever injected into American politics and society. Englishmen acknowledged in 1660 that the ruthless success of the Norman Conquest, the invigorated regime of Henry Tudor, and the nationalism of his granddaughter, Elizabeth, had made monarchical government integral to English national existence.

Charles and his advisers launched a series of colonial initiatives, some worked well, some produced valuable but unforeseen results, and some were disasters. But even after Charles's most ill-conceived plans had unraveled in the aftermath of the short reign of his brother and successor, James II (1685–1688), and after the proprietary colonies that Charles planted had developed in ways in which he could not have foreseen and would not have approved, English possessions in the New World could not have reverted to the drifting and inchoate condition they had known in the years before 1660.

Charles created five proprietary colonies—New York, Carolina, Pennsylvania, East Jersey, and West Jersey. He established the Lords Commissioners of Trade and Plantations and supported the Lords' plans to suspend the charters of the New England colonies and bring Massachusetts (especially) under Crown control. The Exclusion crisis of 1679–1683 was the unsuccessful effort in Parliament to exclude James, Duke of York, from the throne. In that struggle, James's opponents were called "Whigs" and his defenders "Tories." When James became King in 1685, his efforts to establish despotism alienated both his Tory supporters and his Whig enemies, who joined forces to overthrow him in 1688. That struggle taught the colonists indelible lessons about the potency of the value systems represented by the labels "Whig" and "Tory."

The creation of Proprietary colonies under the aegis of the Crown not only promoted settlement and created new provincial administrations, but some of the proprietors drew, perhaps unwittingly, on a body of ideas that were subversive to the authority of the Crown and to traditional notions of hierarchy. These ideas were embodied in the republican political theory of James Harrington's *Oceana* (1656). Harrington lived from 1611 to 1677. He was a companion and close friend of Charles I and may have written *Oceana* as a way of coming to terms with the tragedy of the king's execution in 1649. Yet Harrington was no royalist. He was fascinated with the Renaissance ideal of the republic, or commonwealth, where men, drawing on the wisdom of the past, could construct a new society.

In Carolina, Pennsylvania, and West Jersey, Harrington's vision inspired proprietors to draft constitutional documents to guide political and social development. The Fundamental Constitutions of Carolina (1669), prepared by John Locke, confidant of Anthony Ashley Cooper, Earl of Shaftsbury, proposed a complex division of each of the colony's counties into eight seigniories (each the domain of one of the proprietors), eight baronies, and twenty-four colonies. Although this contrived land system never materialized, the Fundamental Constitutions did shape Carolina's development in subtle but pervasive ways. The document acknowledged the necessity of a balance between aristocratic dominance and popular participation in political life. As Shaftsbury later observed, the Fundamental Constitutions intended that "noe body's power, noe not any of the Proprietors themselves,... is so great as to be able to hurt the meanest [*i.e.*, humblest] man in the country."

William Penn's Frame of Government, drafted for his own proprietary, also reflected Harrington's ideas: a "Senate debating and proposing, the people resolving, and the Magistracy executing," plus the rotation of legislators and their election by the people. But Penn's Frame of Government also grew out of his own Quaker background and his Whiggish beliefs in "life, liberty, and property" under the rule of law. To the Frame of Government, Penn attached "Forty Laws" to be adopted by Pennsylvania's first settlers. They stipulated religious toleration, a broadly based property-owning qualification for voting, trial by jury, and limitation of the death penalty to treason or murder.

Neither Carolina nor Pennsylvania developed politically and socially as the Fundamental Constitutions or the Frame of Government envisioned. Penn quarreled with the Quaker merchants in Philadelphia and gradually lost power to the Assembly, which they dominated; the Carolina proprietors became frustrated by the lack of cooperation from the earliest settlers, especially the large proportion of Barbadian planters who quickly established their preeminence in the infant settlements near Charles Town. These Barbadians were called "Goose Creek men," after their settlement on a tributary of the Cooper River. To thwart the ambitions of the Goose Creek men, the proprietors lavished favor on Anglican settlers, whom they considered to be more closely tied to proprietors in England, and on Protestant dissenters. Both the proprietors and the Goose Creek men sought to curry favor with a large contingent of Carolina's French Huguenot settlers. Though their Calvinism might have led the Huguenots to ally themselves with the Protestant dissenters, the Huguenot's fear of persecution was a stronger force. Therefore, they looked to the Goose Creek faction as a more dependable ally and, in the long run, on assimilation into the Anglican Church as the most prudent religious stance to take. Conflict between the Goose Creek men and the proprietary party became fierce in the 1680s and 1690s. The proprietary party saw their Goose Creek rivals as men who were unwilling to accept restraint from England—perhaps as embodying the commonwealth egalitarianism implicit in the Harringtonian language of the Fundamental Constitutions. John Stewart, a Scottish settler, accused one Goose Creek adversary of being "Metchivell, Hobs, and Lucifer in a Huge lump of Viperish mortality [with] a soull [as] big as a musketo." This insult linked Harrington's visionary commonwealth to Machiavelli's opportunistic political ethics and to Thomas Hobbes's view of the state of nature (expressed in his *Leviathan*, 1651) as a place in which atomized individuals grope blindly for dominion and survival.

New York, the personal proprietary holding of James, Duke of York, following its capture from the Dutch in 1664, should have been the laboratory for instituting an unreconstructed version of the English philosophy of order. For more than a decade and a half, James ruled the colony through appointed governors without authorizing the creation of an elected assembly. However, what one historian calls "a darkening...penumbra of protest" finally persuaded James, in 1682, to authorize an assembly for New York that had the same broad lawmaking authority as legislative bodies in the other English colonies possessed, but with the blunt warning to Governor Thomas Dungan not to sign "any law...raising any public revenue unless express mention is made therein that the [revenue] is levied and granted unto me." Undeterred, the first New York Assembly drafted a boldly libertarian Charter of Libertyes and Priviledges, which: protected the right of "freeholders," or taxpayers, to elect an Assembly; protected the accused from punishment without trial before one's "peers"; and upheld liberty of conscience for all Christians.

James, in concert with the Lords Commissioners of Trade and Plantations, retaliated by incorporating New York into a new supercolony, the Dominion of New England, formed in 1685 when Charles annulled the charters of the New England colonies. In 1686 James placed the entire region under the control of a new military governor, Sir Edmund Andros, who was stationed in Boston and ruled without any elected assembly.

The Glorious Revolution

James's attempt to impose authoritarian colonial government came to naught when he was overthrown in the Glorious Revolution of 1688. His apparent efforts to reimpose Catholicism in England and the birth of a son to his Catholic bride so alienated his former Whig critics and former Tory supporters that they joined to invite the Protestant Prince William of Orange and his wife Mary (James's Protestant daughter) to bring the Dutch army to England. News of William's landing at Torbay, on November 5, 1688, prompted James to vacate the throne and flee to France. (John Dickinson deliberately finished writing his first *Letter of a Pennsylvania Farmer* on November 5, 1767, knowing his readers would recognize the seventy-ninth anniversary of William's landing.)

When news reached Boston in the spring of 1689 that James II had been overthrown, leading Puritan leaders and members of the merchant elite put aside their rivalries, arrested Governor Andros, compelled his small garrison of troops to surrender, and declared their allegiance to William and Mary. William accepted Massachusetts's proffered allegiance, as he did that of Protestant Associators in Maryland who had also seized power, upon the downfall of James, from another heavy-handed colonial regime—the Calvert family. William did not, however, recognize the third rebellious regime to emerge in America as a response to the Glorious Revolution—Jacob Leisler's desperate band of dissidents who seized control of New York. William ordered Leisler deposed.

The Glorious Revolution transformed the concept of order throughout the Anglo-American world. It settled once and for all the question of parliamentary supremacy. And by securing the Protestant succession to the throne (formally codified in the Act of Succession of 1701), the Glorious Revolution insured that absolutism of the kind Louis XIV was then instituting in Catholic France would not develop in the British Isles.

At a deeper level, the Glorious Revolution vindicated the values of empiricism, which had both challenged and tempered the philosophy of order. The leaders of the Glorious Revolution themselves believed in order, and also in a government energetic and powerful enough to protect national security and prosperity. By 1688, however, they had concluded empirically that order depended on conciliating the many segments of society that James II had threatened, attacked, or frightened: Anglican bishops, who, as we shall see, defied James II in 1687; Protestants fearful of Catholic designs and local governments; and those persons who valued the rule of law and feared the presence of a standing royal army in time of peace without the consent of Parliament.

John Locke became the preeminent articulator and interpreter of these hopes and fears. For that reason, and because Locke's political ideas had an even more pervasive impact on colonial thought, Locke's role in the development of English political theory needs careful explication. Though Locke's Fundamental Constitutions of Carolina drew heavily on Harrington's vision of a virtuous state of independent landowners, his political writings in the 1680s, particularly *Two Treatises of Government*, broke new ground. Here Locke vested in individuals, as well as in legal and legislative institutions, the right and duty to preserve liberty based on contractual consent. Lockean contractionalism thus became a powerful alternative to Harrington's republicanism as well as to Hobbes's dark depiction of inherent human conflict.

The essential point about Locke's *Two Treatises* is that he wrote them some time in the early stages of the Exclusion controversy (probably in 1679–1681) as arguments to be used in Shaftsbury's efforts to exclude James from succeeding to the throne. When published in 1690, the *Two Treatises* had been perceived as an elegant, after-the-fact justification of the Glorious Revolution. Instead, Locke's manuscript had already been circulating from hand to hand for ten years, and it made arguments that were more daring and delicate than they were elegant and clever. Locke and his mentor, Shaftsbury, had walked an excruciatingly narrow line between inciting treason and exhorting men of property and substance to preserve the existence of the social order in England. (Not until the 1940s did the Locke scholar, Peter Laslett, discover that the *Two Treatises* dated from the early, rather that the late, 1680s. Since Laslett's new dating, rereading Locke's long, subtle, and discriminating argument has been an immense task of historical reconstruction and philosophical reflection that is still in progress).

Locke's first target in the *Two Treatises* was Sir Robert Filmer, who had been court philosopher for James I during the early seventeenth century and whose major work, *Patriarcha*, was published posthumously in 1680. Filmer argued that all authority is patriarchal, that is, it descends from God the father to earthly kings and thence to male heads of households who govern spouses, children, and servants. To question the authority of a king, in Filmer's mind, was blasphemous. Knowing the Duke of York's predilection for divine-right theory, Locke implicitly equated Filmer's justification of divine-right authority to James's devotion to Catholicism and his ill-concealed ambition to impose Papist despotism on England. Either a divine-right or a Catholic monarch, Locke warned, would lay "a sure and lasting foundation of endless contention and disorder" in England because Protestants would then be forced to choose between forced conversion to Rome or armed resistance against royal designs. The accession of a divine-right papist to the English throne would thus "destroy the bands of government and obedience."

Why? Why would the "bands of obedience" be broken by the ambitions and actions of a tyrannical ruler? Why would the coronation of a king with James's absolutist predilections necessarily spawn "endless contention and disorder"? Locke brilliantly preempted the royalist answer—that none of these things need happen if the people would just remember that they are subject to authority—by appropriating Hobbes's concept of the contract, the implicit bargain exchanging natural liberty for security and order. Locke expanded the benefits of the Hobbesian contract from security and order to life, liberty, and property; he made those benefits into natural human rights, and he asserted the right of the people to overthrow a ruler who violated the terms of the contract.

For Hobbes, the contract was a blanket thrown over the endlessly hostile, aggressive impulses of human beings; for Locke the contract, or compact, was the buffer between the ruler and the ruled. For Locke, authority resided, not in the skill and energy, or even ruthlessness, of the ruler, but in the compact itself, whence it radiated outward, empowering rulers to rule, and enabling subjects to live secure in the knowledge that their liberty and property could not be taken away arbitrarily.

Locke was not just setting up Filmer as a straw man, though discrediting Filmer's theory was crucial to Locke's strategy. In a much larger sense, Locke was trying to determine how people know a political idea to be true. Samuel Parker, the mid–seventeenth-century Anglican critic of religious toleration, whose writings echoed Filmer's, had claimed in 1669 that Protestant dissenters were like "savage

Americans,...rude and boisterous zealots," who were impervious to "calm and sober reason." The only way to rescue such people from religious error, Parker declared, was to "awaken [civil and ecclesiastical] authority" to the threat posed by religious pluralism and to have the might of the state overawe the discontented and restless. Responding to Parker, more than to Filmer, Locke claimed in his *Essay Concerning Human Understanding* (1689) that concurrence with religious teaching requires that people exercise the "faculty of reason," a God-given capacity. Thus there were no innate religious, or for that matter political, ideas. There were only empirical lessons taught by experience and received through the senses.

What made Locke's contract theory so enduring and compelling was the way he fused a historical view of *politics* (based on seventeenth-century struggles against the Stuart monarchy) and a philosophical understanding of *psychology* (based on sensory learning and a God-given freedom to use reason as a means of obtaining secular knowledge and religious belief). How did Locke accomplish this fusion of politics and psychology? John Dunn, a historian of political philosophy who writes extensively on Locke, answers that question by evoking the emotional and cultural context in which Locke lived. "What really threatened the fabric of seventeenth-century English society," writes Dunn, "was not the exuberant self-will of the consciously exploited but the sheer panic of the starving and helpless.... [Locke] understood his society well enough to know that the threat of anarchy came not from [men's] determined and indomitable willfulness but from the destruction of the elementary security of their joyless lives." The Lockean compact enabled people to rise above the desperate fear of arbitrary power and endowed them with the freedom to pursue their own interests, secure in the protection of the rule of law. That confidence, Locke predicted, would become a powerful inducement to the individual to be productive. "God gave the world to men in common, but since he gave it to them for their benefit,...it cannot be supposed that he meant it should always remain common and uncultivated. He gave it to the use of the industrious and rational, ...not to the fancy or covetousness of the quarrelsome and contentious." That design for human society made defense of the contract a supreme test of human self-preservation because, as Dunn paraphrases Locke, "the psychological acceptance of absolute power [was] morally equivalent to suicide" and "no degree of psychological passivity on the part of...subjects can confer legitimacy upon the power of an absolute monarch."

The Anglican Church

The Revolution of 1688–1689 was a traumatic event because the Crown had been the single most important force making England into a single nation, though Parliament, the courts, and the Anglican Church shared that responsibility. The Church of England was supposed to be the moral compass of the nation, and James II's rule had knocked that compass off kilter. At first, the Church had prudently declined to oppose James's apparent design to catholicize England until the king tried to force Magdalen College, at Oxford University, to accept a Catholic president as part of a larger effort to give Catholics access to higher learning. When the fellows of the college resisted, James used an ecclesiastical commission to deprive them of their tenure and income. This attack on property rights terrified property owners throughout England. Then James ordered Anglican clergy to read from their pulpits a Declaration of Toleration for Catholics and dissenters. When seven bishops refused to allow the Declaration to be read in their dioceses, James jailed the bishops, though a Whig judge released them. Gilbert Burnet, Bishop of Salisbury, accompanied the Prince of Orange and his Dutch troops as they marched toward London. Because the king was head of the Church, most Anglican clergy were skittish about breaking their vows of allegiance to the ruler. Most justified breaking their oaths to James and swearing new ones to William and Mary on the grounds that the new rulers were "powers...ordained by God" and thus to be obeyed (Romans 13:1). Others found religious grounds for believing that "nature, reason, and religion" were divinely prescribed bases for moral choice, and that the law of nature required the preservation of society—which only the accession of William and Mary could insure.

Whatever their scruples, churchmen after 1689 felt either the tug of a Tory Anglicanism preserving the exclusive authority of the Church of England or the counter tug of a Whig Anglicanism identifying the Church with the defense of the natural rights of mankind. In 1710, a vehement high Anglican cleric, Dr. Henry Sacheverell, delivered a sensational sermon declaring holy war on everyone in the Church who espoused the right of subjects to resist the authority of a monarch, even a tyrannical one. Following an emotional impeachment trial, the House of Commons briefly imprisoned Sacheverell for his assault against the principle of contract government. Sacheverell was right to be alarmed: the Church of England adapted chameleon-like to Lockean orthodoxy. In a major work on Christian ethics, *The Relative Duties of Parents and Children, Masters and Servants* (1705), Bishop William Fleetwood insisted on obedience to superiors, but in qualified Lockean terms: "Neither father, husband, nor master, nor any superior whatsoever, is to be obeyed *in all things*." The laws of the land and the commands of God, Fleetwood insisted, took precedence over human authorities.

The Anglican Church, though torn between its historic role as a center of power in English society and its chameleon-like ability to adapt itself to political realities, was the most thoughtful and industrious agency seeking to instill English order into colonial society during the first quarter of the eighteenth century. Led by the Reverend Thomas Bray, the Anglican hierarchy and wealthy lay people created: the Society for the Propagation of Christian Knowledge (SPCK) in 1699 to supply Anglican clerics and teachers in the colonies with religious books; the Society for the Propagation of the Gospel in Foreign Parts (SPG) in 1701, to recruit and support missionaries in the far reaches of the empire; and Dr. Bray's Associates in 1723 to send religious teachers among African slaves in the New World.

The pronouncements of these missionary organizations, the experiences of the missionaries who were sent to the colonies, and the controversies surrounding Anglican imperialism express a profoundly held ideological vision of British North America as an uncivilized culture that was hungry for Anglican and English civility, piety, self-control, and cosmopolitan polish. Bray's career illustrates the social roots of this moral and educational enterprise. Rising from humble origins, Bray attended All Souls College, Oxford, on a scholarship, earning his B.A. in 1678. Financial need cut short further study, and three years later he took holy orders and became a curate in his native Shropshire County. His intellectuality and attractive personality caught the eye of an influential landowner in Warwickshire, where he became the vicar of a prestigious parish and began mingling with the powerful and well-connected figures who would become the core supporters of his philanthropic projects. Famed for his teaching, he published his catechetical lectures in 1696, a year after being named by the Bishop of London to be Commissary (*i.e.*, an administrator) of the Anglican Church in Maryland. He delayed moving to America for four years and invested the time organizing a network of financial, recruitment, and administrative support in England for a greatly expanded program of Anglican activity in the colonies. The SPG and SPCK were the major fruits of this effort, and a bequest from a Huguenot philanthropist in Holland, Abel Tassin, the Sieur D'Allone, whom Bray met through William and Mary, established the financial base for the evangelization of colonial slaves—D'Allone's and Bray's pet project. Anglican imperialism sought a radical reformation of the empire—the transformation of its culture by securing for the Church of England a strategic place in colonial life and shaming or inspiring slaveowners into Christianizing their slaves and respecting the human dignity of African bondsmen and bondswomen.

The Anglican vision is hard for modern readers to comprehend because it appears blemished by hypocrisy. In a major sermon in 1711 setting forth the purposes of the SPG, Bishop Fleetwood embraced British mercantilism and colonialism with unabashed fervor, "I would not have any one's zeal for religion (much less my own) so far outrun their judgment...as to cause them to forget that we are a people who live and maintain our selves by *trade*, and that if *trade* is lost, or overmuch discouraged, we are a ruined nation." The SPG urged aristocratic Englishmen to contribute financially to their efforts to evangelize slaves and admonished colonial slaveowners to provide their slaves with religious instruction. The society insisted that Christianity would render slaves obedient and cheerful—and hence become more valuable to their masters and a more productive labor force for the empire.

By so closely linking the salvation of slaves to the preservation of slavery as a labor system, the SPG constructed what historian Jon Butler calls "slaveholder and planter ethics." The Bishop of London, whose jurisdiction included the American colonies, explained in 1727 that "The freedom which Christianity gives is a freedom from the bondage of sin and Satan and from the dominion of men's lusts and passions and inordinate desires; but as to their *outward* condition,... whether bond or free, their being baptised and becoming Christians makes no manner of change in it." Though determined to evangelize

African slaves, Anglican clergy were painfully aware that planter opposition to their ministry could doom it to failure. Francis Le Jau, an early SPG missionary in South Carolina, required each adult slave candidate for baptism to take an oath—in the presence of other slaves and their masters—"that you do not ask for the holy baptism out of any design to free your self from the duty and obedience you owe your master while you live." These gatherings of priests, slaves, and masters at the baptismal font were tense ones. One planter asked his priest apprehensively, "If any of my slaves go to heaven,...must I see them there?" The priest did not record his answer to that question.

The task of the Anglican Church in the colonies was to prepare men and women to live in this world and to bring moderation, self-control, and piety to bear on their social relationships. Anglicans understood this task to be a difficult undertaking. John Tillotson, the premier Anglican theologian of the seventeenth century, agonized over "what a conflict and struggling...the best men [endure] between their inclination and their duty! How hard to reconcile our practice with our knowledge,...to be...either so wise or so good as he ought!" Thus the task of the Church of England, as a guarantor of the peace of the kingdom and prosperity of the empire was, as one SPG sermon declared, "to dispose men to everything productive of the common good: to justice and veracity,...duty and love in the several relations of life,...to mildness, charity, and compassion,...to sobriety and industry, and to that joyful hope of a better world which is our truest direction ...in every stage of our journey through this [life]." The hope of eternal life was important because it encouraged the living of a moral life, meaning an obedient life, here and now.

Conclusion: Colonial Disorder and Anglican Moral Prescription

Anglicanism was a sensitive barometer of cultural change in the British Empire and especially of the degradation of English habits of order. The SPCK distributed in the colonies thousands of copies of a book, *The Whole Duty of Man*, which taught acceptance of one's assigned place in the social order. The colonies, Bishop Richard Secker told the SPG in 1740, were preeminently a place where Anglican social conservatism could bring healing to a society beset by the "corruptions of Christianity" spread by illiterate and unlicensed dissenting clergymen.

A vigorous underclass of unregulated preachers and irregular congregations in America was dangerous because it pulled society apart rather than knitting it together with respect for a constituted authority. The task of the Church of England, declared Timothy Cutler, one of the earliest New England Congregationalist clergy to defect to Anglicanism, was to instill into the colonial mind an understanding of the purposes of government, the need for political authority imperious to "entreaty," "flattery," "friendship," or "terror," in short, unaffected by the turbulence of a pluralistic and still immature colonial culture.

Anglicanism sought to discipline and humanize colonial society by teaching that society itself was a web of connections. Samuel Johnson of Connecticut, who with Cutler was another Congregationalist defector to the Anglican Church, devoted his life to the study of philosophy and religion. In a treatise written sometime in the 1760s, he surveyed the question of how God intended sinful people to live together. The variety of climates and environments in the world, Johnson said, required men to develop a variety of skills and ways of doing business: "So God hath given men no less various and different geniuses and different turns of mind and endowed them with a wonderful diversity of faculties and inclinations by...which they are designed ...to promote...the general good of the whole.... In this dependent situation,...he must be solicitous for the weal and prosperity of everyone else." Because each individual occupied a rank in society below some of his fellows and above others, Johnson's social ethics included acceptance of one's place, as well as one's function, in society. Social interconnectedness was therefore an integral part of the divine plan.

The Anglican view of reality mirrored two generations of change in English history. Between the Restoration of Charles II in 1660 and the death of the last Stuart ruler, Queen Anne, in 1714, the British nation and its empire experienced irrevocable changes. Charles II's ambitious proprietary colonies invigorated the effort to colonize North America. The effort to centralize control of the colonies, begun under Charles II and accelerated during the brief reign of James II, floundered because the nation was deeply divided on the question of how much authority the Crown possessed and because the colonists had learned during the first century of settlement to enjoy a high degree of autonomy.

When James II's own rash actions provoked his overthrow in 1688, Englishmen realized how much they had learned about the nature of power and authority from the upheavals and tensions of the sixteenth and seventeenth centuries. They drew on Hobbes, who had the courage and insight to see that society itself was a dangerous place, and on Locke, who had the moral insight to realize that the evils of this world were a blessing as well as a curse because they required men to take personal responsibility for the well-being of the state. As demanding as that was for Englishmen in the well-ordered English countryside, it was more difficult for colonists struggling to subdue a wilderness, to enrich the economy of the parent state, and to enrich themselves as well.

The Anglican Church recognized the moral dilemmas faced by England and by the colonists. The Church implored Englishmen to finance the Anglican evangelization of America and beseeched the colonists to curb their ambitions, to soften their exploitation of the Indians and their slaves, to accept a subordinate place in the empire, and to endure evils intrinsic to a developing and resource-rich society until such time as God's Providence solved those problems. The growth and prosperity of the empire during the first decades of the eighteenth century depended heavily on this Augustan ideology of order and constraint.

William Hogarth, *An Election Entertainment* (1755).

CHAPTER THREE

A Mature Metropolitan System and Its Social Costs, 1714–1773

DURING the reigns of the first two Hanoverian kings, George I (1714–1727) and George II (1727–1760), Great Britain became a great metropolitan power. Its commercial and naval power extended around the world. Its political and legal institutions possessed the strength and capacity to govern not only the British Isles but also a far-flung empire. Far from imbuing British statesmen and men of affairs with self-confidence, this national good fortune filled them with apprehension. The accession of George III (1760–1820) did not inaugurate an era of *Pax Britannica*; on the contrary, the rigidities and excesses that had developed over the preceding four decades made imperial institutions clumsy and self-serving.

The strife and instability of the seventeenth century had hung over eighteenth-century England like a cloud, one which had grown more ominous with the threat that James II or his son might return to power following the reigns of William and Mary or their successor, Anne. Not until the accession of the Hanoverian George I in 1714 and the suppression in 1715 of a Scottish uprising in the Stuart Pretender's behalf (the Jacobite cause) was the Protestant succession secure.

Reflecting these tensions during Anne's reign had been the fierce jockeying for power by Whig and Tory factions, with Whigs favoring and Tories opposing the aggressive prosecution of the war against Louis XIV and the toleration of Protestant dissenters. Whig-Tory rivalry and Jacobite conspiracies thus had kept England and Scotland astir from the 1690s until after 1715. The union of England and Scotland into the kingdom of Great Britain in 1707 only had begun the work of stabilizing English politics and stimulating the Scottish economy.

Walpole and Salutary Neglect

When Robert Walpole became the king's first minister in 1721, he set out to devise a political system that could put an end to these troubles. To quell the thriving competition between Whigs and Tories, Walpole capitalized on the fact that leading Tories had been discredited by their part in the Jacobite plots of 1715. Henceforth, a Whig supremacy—a coalition of Whig factions representing nearly all of the landed aristocracy and merchant and financial elites—dominated Parliament and governed the realm. To maintain consensus and calm, Walpole assumed the responsibility for insuring that the benefits of aristocratic government and commercial prosperity were widely distributed. Under Walpole's system, the foremost task of Parliament was the enactment of private bills to assist individuals of wealth and influence with legal, inheritance, and business problems. The most potent guarantees of political stability in Walpole's system were patronage and bureaucracy. Increasingly, the importance of trade and naval power required a burgeoning bureaucracy. The Board of Trade—which replaced the Lords Commissioners of Trade and Plantations in 1696—and the Admiralty were the agencies responsible for preserving commercial power and prosperity. But the most potent value of the bureaucracy was its capacity to provide livelihood for hundreds of supplicants for office. Walpole kept parliamentary factions under control by doling out offices to the friends, relatives, and political supporters of prominent members of Parliament.

Bureaucratic Imperialism

Cynical, pragmatic, successful, and down to earth though it was, Walpole's system nonetheless reflected a mature, metropolitan world view. And within the bowels of the bureaucracy, a new generation of professional administrators converted this world view into an ideology—a mixture of the older philosophy of order, which they had inherited from the seventeenth century, and the new regime-oriented values of the British parliamentary, bureaucratic, and royal insiders, who can collectively be labeled "the court."

Central to the thinking of imperial insiders was the elation they felt over recent political and military victories: seeing Britain suddenly emerge after the wars against Louis XIV as a world power. Martin Bladen, a British bureaucrat, also emphasized the benefits of empire: "the importance of the British [colonies] in America,...the manufactures we send them, the produce we bring home from thence for our own consumption,...the commodities they furnish us...for...re-export,...and the balance we gain by their trade." This wealth and national economic power were so great, Bladen explained in 1739, that "the general voice of the people" had called upon the Crown to enter into war with Spain and eventually with France "for the preservation of it." This description of the benefits of empire demonstrated how central mercantilism had become to Britain's self-confidence and its exercise of national power.

Jeopardizing this beneficial relationship of Britain to its colonies was the lamentable fact, as Bladen and three of his colleagues wrote to George I in 1721, that, although "the laws and constitutions of your Majesty's colonies are copied from those of Great Britain, [they] fall short of them in many particulars." These included the generous terms under which charter and proprietary colonies had gained from the Crown title to vast tracts of land, the use "pirates and outlaws" had made of proprietary colonies as sanctuaries, the impossibility of collecting more than a fraction of the quitrents due from land grants in royal colonies, and the failure of Parliament to preserve the "woods of America" as "an inexhaustable store for the Royal Navy."

That Bladen and his colleagues felt it necessary to tell the king that the organization of the empire was defective reflected what Jack P. Greene has called "a new tone of administration" under Walpole of "leniency" toward the colonies and the increasingly mixed groups of European and British settlers gathered in America. When Governor Francis Nicholson of South Carolina cracked down on smuggling by the Huguenot merchant, Benjamin Godin, and the Huguenot emigre community in London complained to Walpole, Nicholson received this rebuke from Walpole's secretary: "The dissenters are a powerful body [in Britain] and will, you may believe, be always ready to represent [*i.e.*, protest] any injury done their brethren abroad.... It is certainly best to keep up friendship and good neighbor[liness] among the inhabitants of a colony...where government should be as mild and easy as possible, [in order to encourage] people to settle under it." Colonial governors thus felt caught between "Scylla and Charybdis"—literally a rock and a hard place in the *Odyssey*—between losing control of restive colonies and alienating their provinces through tough enforcement of law and policy.

Governing mildly was extremely difficult, requiring as it did restraint, prudence, and conciliation of colonial leaders. The existence of legislative assemblies in every colony enabled colonial leaders to become skilled and resourceful legislators. In a piecemeal fashion, the assemblies won not only legislative control but also control of the purse—the powers to tax and appropriate public funds and periodically to print paper money. Several assemblies went further and sought to control the executive branches of their respective colonial governments by setting the fees that public officials charged for performing their duties.

A fierce dispute between Virginia and imperial officials in the early 1750s erupted when Lieutenant Governor Robert Dinwiddie, backed by the Board of Trade, announced that henceforth the fee for issuing land grants in the colony would be a pistole, a Spanish coin worth 16 shillings 10 pence—a substantial sum that exceeded the value of many small land grants. The Virginia House of Burgesses objected to the "Pistole Fee" as an infringement on its traditional power of the purse, and the whole dispute was argued by lawyers for the governor and the Burgesses in an emotional hearing before the Privy Council in London on June 18, 1754.

The lawyers' briefs in that hearing articulated clearly the mindsets of the parties to the controversy. Counsel for the Burgesses emphasized Dinwiddie's greed, his abrupt disregard for the assembly's traditional power to set the fees of royal officeholders, and the ominous new tone that the Pistole Fee dispute had injected into imperial administration. "If your Lordships do not restrain officers [like Dinwiddie] within due bounds," he said, "they will abuse their authority." Dinwiddie's lawyer declared that the governor was simply carrying out the King's instructions. "As the King is absolute proprietor of these lands," he insisted, "he may act by his substitute [Dinwiddie]...and without" being accused of "oppression, extortion, or exaction, pass grants of land in this colony upon what terms he pleases." What threatened the well-being of the empire, the brief for the governor continued, was the Virginia planters' "inordinate and boundless...lust" for lands, while insisting that it was they who should set the fees they paid for those lands. This greed and arrogance was "the latent seed of a distemper" that bordered on rebelliousness. The Privy Council upheld Dinwiddie and the Crown—an early signal that the Crown and the Board of Trade had determined that the piecemeal accumulation of power by the Virginia House of Burgesses should come to an end.

The British cabinet ministers, who favored the relaxed administration of the colonies, what Edmund Burke later labelled "salutary neglect," and the bureaucrats who fretted over colonial autonomy shared a common belief that patronage was the cement of the political system under the Hanoverians. Patronage brought political stability, and it gave individuals with powerful patrons a reward for their loyalty. This mixture of societal benefits and personal gratification generated wealth, a self-confidence bordering on arrogance, and a frank celebration in the display of power at the highest levels of the British establishment. Walpole was the embodiment of these achievements and this excess. His biographer and the foremost authority on eighteenth-century English Politics, J. H. Plumb, concludes that

> excellent administrative ability, an outstanding parliamentary skill, [and] the unshakable favor of the King...gave Walpole an eminence in English life unparalleled since Burleigh [Elizabeth's great adviser]. [These abilities] brought great crowds of sycophants to his door [and] such sycophancy did not leave his character unmarked.... His whole manner of life bred detestation wherever he went. He paraded his wealth with ever greater ostentation. He bought pictures at reckless prices, wallowed in the extravagance of Houghton [his estate], deluged his myriad guests with rare food and costly wine; his huge ungainly figure sparkled with diamonds and flashed with satin. And he gloried in his power.

Opposition Thinkers

TRENCHARD AND GORDON

This image of bloated, selfish power provoked an explosive ideological reaction. The most prominent figures in the opposition to Walpole's system—which they called "Robinocracy," in a jeering allusion to Walpole's first name—were two obscure journalists, John Trenchard and his protege Thomas Gordon. In their short-lived magazines, *The Independent Reflector* and *Cato's Letters*, Trenchard and Gordon articulated a profound libertarian fear that religious and civil liberty were as endangered in the 1720s as they had been in the early 1680s. Indeed, liberty was perhaps more endangered now because the illicit use of money rewarded oppressors and implicated thousands of officeholders, contractors, and financial opportunists with pieces of the action. "Luxury," Trenchard and Gordon wrote in *Cato's Letters*, "is the harbinger of a dying state." Rulers and their cronies who had bloated appetites would do anything to maintain their precarious position atop the social order: make trading alliances with "open enemies, suspected friends, or dangerous neighbors," or dispense public offices "without any regard for qualifications" other than "a stupid alacrity to do what they are bid." Corrupt or incompetent officeholders had the further propensity to provoke "disaffection" among the people, thus providing a pretext for "new oppression."

Trenchard and Gordon were appealing to Englishmen to return to the principles of the Glorious Revolution. They condemned the Whigs of the 1690s for allowing the Crown to become engorged with revenues and administrative authority associated with a standing army, for allowing the Church of England to retain a privileged place in the political order, and for failing to return England to the pure commonwealth that had existed before 1660. They traced the rise and fall of Stuart despotism and its replacement by a Whig regime contaminated with lingering vices.

Englishmen, "Cato" warned, had neglected the study of human nature and society. "The first principle of power is property, and every man will have his share of [power] in proportion as he enjoys...and makes use of that property, [as long as] violence does not interpose." Property could not be held securely in a society where nobility and the monarchy contended for power and a desperate struggle for illicit political eminence plunged the society into tumult.

But whereas principles of constitutional government restrained the power-hungry and desperate from violence and intrigue, property ownership and economic advancement could become the glue that holds society together. The good society, "Cato" said, did not depend on human virtue. On the contrary, "ambition, avarice, and vanity, and other human passions" ruled human behavior. But political and religious liberty enabled selfish, passionate, and contentious individuals to live together in harmony because, "All men are born free. No man has power over his own life or to dispose of his own religion and cannot consequently transfer the power of either to anybody else, much less can he give away the lives and liberties, religion or acquired property of his posterity, who will be born as free as himself."

Credited by Robbins, Bailyn, and Pocock with being the great popularizers of Harringtonian republicanism in Walpolean England, Trenchard and Gordon were also—as Ronald Hamowy has recently demonstrated—Lockean individualists. Locke's *Two Treatises* were the foundation of their political education. "By liberty," Cato declared, "I understand the power which every man has over his actions, and his right to enjoy the fruits of his labor, art, and industry, as far as by it he hurts not the society or any members of it....When there is liberty, there are encouragements to labor because people labor for themselves." Thus Trenchard and Gordon intermingled Lockean assumptions about liberty with republican strictures against corruption and tyranny in much the same way as would American Revolutionary thinkers, and some English radicals, a generation later.

The Independent Whig and *Cato's Letters* marked a pivotal moment in the history of the idea of liberty. They echoed a seventeenth-century republican tradition created by writers like John Milton, Andrew Marvell, Algernon Sidney, Marchamont Needham, Henry Neville, Gilbert Burnet, and Robert Molesworth. With Bishop Benjamin Hoadly, they denounced the imperious divine-right presumptions of the high church party in the Church of England. And they anticipated the movement that, in the 1760s and 1770s, would form around John Wilkes—informed by the writings of republicans of the 1760s like James Burgh and Catherine Macaulay—to demand the reform of parliamentary elections. All three of these groups of opposition thinkers contributed to the political education of American Revolutionary leaders, and the earlier ones were especially influential in the drafting of Revolutionary state constitutions in 1776. When asked by other American leaders for guidelines on how to draft a constitution, the bookish John Adams pointed first to the writings of "Sidney, Harrington, Lock[e], Milton, Needham, Neville, Burnet, [and] Hoadly."

Why did these exotic republican theorists become such a luminous source of guidance for opposition politicians in the Anglo-American world during the eighteenth century? The names Harrington and Locke provide part of the answer. Harrington brought political theory in England to a new level of conceptual elegance and, by drawing on the Florentine republican tradition of Machiavelli, applied Renaissance thought to the social and political crises of England. Locke built on Harrington by synthesizing in his contract theory a century of parliamentary, Protestant, and legal ideas about the liberty of the subject.

SIDNEY

Algernon Sidney adds a new ingredient to Adams's self-education in constitutionalism. Falsely accused of conspiring to assassinate Charles II during the Exclusion crisis, and hanged, drawn, and quartered in 1683, Sidney left behind him a formidable body of writings about the tyrannical proclivities of pro-Catholic, high church Anglican, and divine-right Stuart forces in Restoration England. As Alan Craig Houston argues in *Algernon Sidney and the Republican Heritage in England and America* (1991), the most recent major study of Anglo-American political thought, Sidney joined the classical and Renaissance tradition of virtue and "self-affirmation" to "the Christian virtue of self-denial:...Sidney's theory was not intended to facilitate 'the release of personal virtue' [but] to enable citizens to achieve common goals and to protect their liberty."

"Being ready to dye," Sidney wrote from the Tower of London shortly before his execution, "I leave this testimony...that...I...endeavoured to uphold the common right of mankind, the lawes of this land, and the true Protestant religion against corrupt principles, arbitrary power and Popery; I do now willingly lay down my life for the same." Sidney's writing and his serenity in the face of death combined to make him the supreme libertarian hero of the early modern world.

NEVILLE AND MOLESWORTH

Other veterans of Cromwell's "Commonwealth" regime continued the search for a theoretical solution to the problem of tyranny. Sidney's contemporary, Henry Neville, published *Plato Redivivus* in 1680, which, like Harrington, stressed the connection between independent property owners and virtuous political judgment but, unlike Harrington, advocated "redressing" the English monarchy to make it serve the needs of the people. The great poet John Milton, who had held office under Oliver Cromwell, continued to lend his literary fame to the republican cause by defending the execution of Charles I and by his eloquent condemnation of censorship. During the eighteenth century, Marchamont Needham's *The Excellencie of a Free State* (1656) influenced the French enlightenment concept of progress.

In the 1690s Viscount Robert Molesworth drew on all of these seventeenth-century "Commonwealthmen" when, from exile in Denmark, he wrote *An Account of Denmark*, which depicted the betrayal of liberty and the rise of an oppressive state church and standing army, ostensibly in Denmark but obviously referring to England. Molesworth became the guru of a cluster of young men—among them John Toland, Charles Devenant, and John Trenchard—who during the reign of Queen Anne called themselves "True Whigs," as opposed to the Whig factions that had struggled for power and finally ascended to political dominance under Walpole.

HOADLY

What Molesworth did for the "True Whigs," Benjamin Hoadly, Bishop of Bangor, did for the vanguard of rationalist Anglican clergymen inspired by John Locke's *Essay on Toleration* and politically aligned with the supporters of the Glorious Revolution. Hoadly and the other Anglican Whigs were politicized by the trial of Dr. Sacheverell and their discovery that doctrines of divine right continued to command a wide following within the Church of England. Hoadly attacked these doctrines with scorn, energy, and vituperation and earned a reputation as "the best hated clergyman of the century amongst his own order." The people, Hoadly felt confident, did not need the sort of "bridle" that high churchmen wanted them to wear.

For Hoadly, repudiating the hierarchical power of kings and bishops also had the breathtaking consequence of destroying the authority of the church to make authoritative statements about faith. "Christ... is the sole law giver to his subjects, and...the sole judge of their behavior in affairs of conscience and eternal salvation." Consequently, "neither our Lord nor his disciples...formed any exact system of morality" beyond "the great and universal law of reason." Thus radical Whigs within the Anglican hierarchy repudiated the authority of human institutions over the rational judgment of individuals.

By bringing the libertarian beliefs of seventeenth- and early eighteenth-century English commonwealthmen to bear on the issues of the 1720s and 1730s, Trenchard and Gordon constructed a new way of viewing the structure of politics around the concepts of the "court" and the "country." The court encompassed the insiders within the political system of patronage and preferment. The country was the place from which disinterested patriots observed this concentration of power and privilege and assessed its impact on the well-being of the nation.

BOLINGBROKE

The claim of geographical and moral separation from the temples of power attracted a formidable and unlikely recruit to the country party, Henry St. John, Viscount Bolingbroke. St. John had been the ablest Tory politician during the reign of Anne and was responsible as secretary of state from 1710 to 1713 for negotiating the far-sighted and generous terms of the Treaty of Utrecht, which ended the wars between Britain and Louis XIV. Implicated in the Jacobite conspiracy to prevent the Hanoverian succession to the throne, St. John fled to France to avoid imprisonment and was convicted by a bill of attainder. During the early 1720s, St. John, now Lord Bolingbroke, skillfully appealed to the gentry landowners, whose economic position had steadily worsened during the half century following 1688. What particularly outraged these men was a financial scandal in 1720 known as the "South Sea bubble," a shady and very risky investment scheme in the Isthmus of Panama, which Walpole and other ministers had—in return for payoffs—endorsed. When the South Sea Company collapsed, hundreds of investors were ruined. In anonymous writings, Bolingbroke and his allies castigated the government for its corrupt involvement in the scandal. Then Bolingbroke bribed a German duchess in order to gain access to the king, whom he flattered with ingratiating letters. Pressured by George I, Walpole agreed that Bolingbroke should be allowed to return home, but on the condition that he abstain from involvement in politics. Bolingbroke complied by restricting himself to writing works on political theory, which were, however, critical of the new political order.

Between them, Bolingbroke, Trenchard, and Gordon recruited into opposition politics journalists, artisans, a few eccentric aristocrats who read "Cato's" letters, and the far more conservative Tory gentry, to whom Bolingbroke appealed. With an instinct for the jugular surpassing that of the radical Whigs, Bolingbroke asserted that "the power of money, as the world is now constituted, is real power." The new national debt, the rising level of taxation, the exchange of contracts and favors for money, and the use of patronage to reward the supporters of the government all created a new "unnatural state of society" where power flowed to "persons who possess revenue beyond the immediate effects of their industry.... These are men who have no connexion with the state [that is, with society], who can enjoy their revenue in any part of the globe in which they chuse to reside, who will naturally bury themselves in the capital [London] or [other] great cities." The radical result of the Walpolean system of monied politics was to destroy the traditional institutions of "nobility, gentry, and family." By detaching wealth from land and property and giving it liquidity, "stocks can be transferred in an instant, and being in such a fluctuating state, will seldom be transmitted...from father to son." Under these conditions, liberty itself was in peril. Instead of the traditional leadership by "the great and rich families in the several counties, cities, and boroughs of England," power now resided in a clique of ministers, financiers, and courtiers. Thus did Bolingbroke analyze British politics in the late 1720s.

Over the next two decades he refined and extended his political theory, and in 1749 he published "The Idea of a Patriot King," in which appeared a collection of other essays entitled *Letters on the Spirit of Patriotism.* When George III seemed to change overnight from the pleasing young ruler he had been in 1763 to a usurper of colonial liberty, colonial leaders turned to Bolingbroke for an explanation of what had happened to their rights as Englishmen. Bolingbroke argued that the tie of the monarchy to British landowners—the aristocracy and the gentry—was a far older and more legitimate function of kingship than the Hanoverians' role as heads of a parliamentary faction of royal officeholders known as the "King's Friends," with their close working relationship with ministers like Walpole or his successor, Henry Pelham, and later, the Duke of Newcastle. Bolingbroke's concept of monopoly raised hopes by 1760 that George III would rise above parties and select ministers on the basis of their fidelity to the national interest:

> The true image of a free people, governed by a Patriot King, is that of a patriarchal family where the head and all the members are united by one common interest and animated by one common spirit, and where if any are perverse enough to have another [interest or spirit], they will soon be borne down by the superiority of those who have the same...and [who] confirm the unity of the...state.

If Bolingbroke sounds a little like Robert Filmer in his celebration of patriarchal society, the reason is not hard to find. Bolingbroke did not agree with Filmer's divine-right philosophy, and he preferred Locke's contractual explanation of the subjects' rights. But Bolingbroke did not accept Locke's basic principle that natural rights were lodged in each individual. Nor did he believe that the contract preceded the creation of the state. He scoffed at the notion of "strolling savages" who would agree to accept restraints on their aggressive behavior, and he insisted that order rather than liberty was the purpose of the contract:

> The union...between prince and people neither can nor ought to subsist on other terms than those of good government on one part and of gratitude and expectation on the other.

Machiavelli could not have said it better. By fortifying opposition political theory with a much more rigorous political philosophy, and by acknowledging the relevance of Renaissance republicanism to eighteenth-century British life, Bolingbroke helped to create a tradition of libertarian thought distinct from Lockean liberalism. It was, paradoxically, a republicanism that was more radical than Locke's and yet also much more conservative.

Scottish Moral Thought

HUME

Still more influential in colonial America than the commonwealthmen or Bolingbroke were the writings of a second major group of opposition thinkers—the Scottish moral philosophers known as the "Common Sense" school. And standing beside them was Scotland's premier Enlightenment philosopher, David Hume, who, like Bolingbroke in

England, was a powerful conservative critic of his fellow rationalists. He was a radical empiricist who doubted every proposition unsupported by concrete evidence.

To understand the Scottish contribution to the discussion of power requires an appreciation of Hume's probing insights into history and then an examination of the way in which Scottish moral philosophers countered Hume's skepticism. Hume was a major figure in the Enlightenment, and his *Dialogues on Natural Religion* provided the most cogently reasoned Enlightenment case for questioning the existence of God. Though he approved of the Glorious Revolution, he cautioned that there was nothing permanent about constitutional protections of liberty. Folly, "barbarism" and the unpredictable forces at work just beneath the surface of political life, he warned, constantly jeopardized civility. But while he scanned the record of human error and irrationality, Hume had a sharp eye for the accidental, unintended good fortune that sustained civilization in spite of itself.

Two of his observations had special relevance for America. "Tis on opinion only that government is founded," Hume observed. No amount of force could persuade the many to be governed by the few. Edmund S. Morgan argues that by "opinion" Hume meant those mythic beliefs, such as the divine right of kings or the sovereignty of the people, that undergird a whole system of government. The transition from the myth of kingship to the myth of democracy occurred between 1660 and 1800 in the Anglo-American world, and thus Hume boldly justified the possibility of a sweeping change in politics. Hume's other contribution to the ideological origins of the American republic was his suggestion that republican government would work better in a large than in a small geographical setting, because an "extended republic" would provide a larger talent pool of legislators and other public officials. That insight almost certainly inspired James Madison in 1784 to envision a new constitution that lodged powers over taxation, trade regulation, debt, and a money supply in a national government.

HUTCHESON

Hume's greatest contribution to Scottish political thought was his religious skepticism and his strict empiricism, which goaded a generation of Scottish intellectuals to construct a theory of knowledge consistent with the nation's Calvinist heritage and an intuitive sense about human capability. The founder of this Common Sense approach to knowing and being was Francis Hutcheson, the son of a Presbyterian minister, who taught at the University of Glasgow from 1730 until his death in 1746. In his *System of Moral Philosophy*, Hutcheson constructed a new understanding of the working of the human mind. His theory drew on Calvinist sources, the commonwealth writings of Harrington and Molesworth, and an Aristotelian understanding of politics as a social endeavor. He located propensities in mankind of sociability, cooperation, and humanitarianism that education ought to awaken and a public-spirited culture that ought to channel constructive activity.

Boldly and consistently libertarian, Hutcheson argued that the colonies should eventually become independent, that religious belief could never be coerced, and that the people always possessed the right to resist a tyrannical government. "As the end of all political unions must be the general good of those thus united [Hutcheson wrote of colonial systems],...if the plan of the mother country is changed by force, or degenerates by degrees from a safe, mild, and general power to a severe and absolute one, [the colonists] are not bound to continue in their subjection." Written sometime in the 1740s and published after his death, those words defined the autonomy and eventual liberty of the colonies as a moral imperative more clearly than any other piece of British republican writing.

Hutcheson's students and proteges produced a brilliant body of teaching and writing extending and amplifying his line of inquiry. Thomas Reid, in his *Essays on Human Understanding* (1764) criticized Locke and Hume for limiting the work of the mind to separate sensations and perceptions. The mind, Reid wrote, reasonably constructs beliefs because it ascribes meaning to what it observes and learns. As long as reason did not refute the generalizing and systematizing conclusions of human thought, he argued, those conclusions possessed intellectual authority independent of the specific sensations and perceptions. Knowledge, according to Reid, was not an accumulation of sensations and perceptions; it was the ideas that sensory learning suggested to the mind and that particular facts and clusters of facts validated.

This concept of learning made the mind itself, rather than the mind as receiver of sense data, the vehicle for civilizing and humanizing the world. It also made rhetoric the critical skill for human interaction.

Hugh Blair was the Scottish moral philosopher whose ideas about rhetoric most powerfully influenced Americans in the early nineteenth century. Blair moved away from classical Roman ideas about persuasive oratory as a legislative skill, toward appreciating oratory as an exercise in moral solidarity. "Without possessing...virtuous affections in a strong degree," he taught his students, "no man can attain eminence in the sublime parts of oratory. He must feel what a good man feels if he expects to move or to interest mankind. [He must feel] the ardent sentiments of honour, virtue, magnanimity and publick spirit."

DUNCAN

The Scottish rhetorician William Duncan advocated a system for the imparting of "self-evident" truths by which the speaker would implant ethical appeals into both his major and minor premises so that the audience would simultaneously concur with the logic of the argument and intuitively feel its moral force. Jefferson's Declaration of Independence adhered closely to this model:

> Men are endowed by their creator [major premise]...deriving their just powers from the consent of the governed [minor premise]...the right of the people to alter or abolish...government destructive of these ends [conclusion].

SMITH

Hutcheson's most brilliant student, Adam Smith, had an enormous, but often misunderstood, influence on the concept of freedom. His *Inquiry into the Wealth of Nations* (1776) identified laws of supply and demand that made the market place the determinant of the creation and the distribution of wealth. Thus a governmental policy of *laissez faire* toward the economy was the best way to produce human happiness for all producers and consumers. When Smith wrote *The Wealth of Nations*, he assumed that his readers would have already read his first book, *A Theory of Moral Sentiments* (1759). In this work, Smith identified conscience as the hidden hand guiding human affairs.

Smith would have been bemused by what scholars now call "*Das Adam Smith Problem*:...the...difficulty of reconciling the sympathetic and benevolent ethic of [his] *Theory of Moral Sentiments* with the selfish or self-interested ethic in the *Wealth of Nations.*" For a Scottish moral philosopher like Smith, there was no contradiction. The human mind was a microcosm of the moral order of the universe; therefore human nature may be self-centered, but the communal, social condition of human life impinges on the egocentric quality of human choices in ways almost indistinguishable from self-interest.

These Scottish ideas had a special potency in colonial and Revolutionary America. As Bernard Bailyn and John Clive suggested in an essay written in 1957 for the 250th anniversary of the union of England and Scotland, Scotland and British North America were both cultural provinces of England. Both were uncomfortable with their cultural backwardness as measured against the standards of the metropolitan center in London, and yet at the same time both felt morally superior to the somewhat corrupt and complacent English giant. During the decades following the union of England and Scotland, Scottish banks had pioneered in underwriting the Glasgow export trade, and Scottish merchants had penetrated deeply into colonial markets.

Witherspoon

Much of the British emigration to America in the eighteenth century came either directly from Scotland or from Ulster in northern Ireland, a Scottish enclave. In 1767 the Presbyterian College of New Jersey at Princeton called the leading evangelical clergyman in Scotland, John Witherspoon, as its president.

Witherspoon's reputation for piety and eloquence arose from his leadership of the evangelical wing of the Church of Scotland, and in particular from his ability to castigate and caricature the rationalist clergy and laity who looked to Hutcheson and moral philosophy for their bearings. But once in America, Witherspoon became the great exponent of Scottish moral philosophy because it served to unify American Presbyterianism and imbue American patriotism with Christian purpose. James Madison, Princeton class of 1772, probably encountered Hume's ideas about the vulnerability and the potentiality of republican government as Witherspoon's student. Even more important, he learned from Witherspoon's lectures on moral philosophy that "it is folly to expect that the state should be upheld by the integrity of [the officials] managing it." Therefore the collective virtue of the citizenry had to serve as a counterpoise, offsetting the self-seeking actions of individuals. That insight from Scottish moral philosophy would become a central tenet of Madison's contribution to *The Federalist.*

Thus Scottish moral philosophy provided American colonial opposition political leaders with an alternative to the republicanism of the English country party, and both the country ideology and Scottish Common Sense differed from Lockean liberalism. English and Scottish republicans emphasized the communal nature of the defense of liberty and the social character of virtue, while Lockean contractualism made the natural libertarian rights of the individual the cutting edge of opposition politics. Taken together, these three traditions—English radicalism, Scottish moralism, and the older Lockean contractualism—were the primary sources of American Revolutionary ideology.

British Radicals in the Reign of George III

WILKES

Heightening the appeal of each of these ideological traditions in America—but especially of English radicalism—was the rise to prominence in the 1760s and early 1770s of John Wilkes. In 1763 Wilkes attacked the Earl of Bute, the King's chief minister and intimate friend, in his essay *North Britain Number 45*, a title alluding to the Scottish Jacobite rebellion of 1745. Parliament used the arcane procedure of issuing a general warrant to try to imprison Wilkes, who fled to France. Returning to England in 1768, Wilkes won election to the House of Commons only to be expelled and then jailed at the express desire of the king, on the grounds that *North Britain Number 45* was libelous and his *Essay on Woman* (1763) obscene. Repeated reelection to Parliament and expulsion from the Commons in 1768–1769 made Wilkes a national hero. Nearly a quarter of the qualified voters in the kingdom signed petitions asking Parliament to allow him to take his seat. Aristocratic figures hostile to the governments headed by the Duke of Grafton (1768–1770) and Lord North (1770–1782) formed the Society of Gentlemen Supporters of the Bill of Rights to embarrass the establishment. And, as we have seen in Chapter One, colonial politicians from Boston to Charleston rallied to Wilkes's cause.

Colonial newspapers followed Wilkes's career closely. They noted that he was steeped in commonwealth ideas, and they compared the general warrants used against him to the Writs of Assistance—new, stringent search warrants that were used by Crown officials against suspected smugglers in Boston in 1762. During Wilkes's imprisonment in 1769, the British radical, the Reverend Horne Tooke, played on Wilkes's martyrdom and kept London in uproar and delight by organizing prison visitations. When the New York activist, Alexander McDougall, was jailed in 1770 for seditious libel against the acting governor, Cadwallader Colden, his supporters hailed him as the "American Wilkes" and provided him the visitations of forty-five virgins who sang him forty-five songs. (One of McDougall's supporters claimed with a straight face that the prisoner's pleasure was not lessened by the fact that each of the virgins was forty-five years of age.)

MACAULAY AND BURGH

Wilkes eventually became Lord Mayor of London and faded as a radical symbol. But the rich subculture of radicalism that had formed in the 1760s and 1770s continued to jeopardize political stability in England and to inspire radicals in America. Catherine Macaulay, in her six-volume *History of England* (1761–1781), sympathized with the goals of Oliver Cromwell's interregnum government and advocated a thorough reform of British elections and government. Her contemporary, James Burgh, produced a series of books that decried Britain's corrupt and unresponsive political system and applied commonwealth standards of virtue to the England of George III. Almost unknown until Caroline Robbins rediscovered him in the 1950s, Burgh's last and most important work, *Political Disquisitions* (1774), was one that Jefferson recommended, along with the works of Adam Smith, Montesquieu, and Locke, as essential reading on politics.

Burgh was a transitional figure who echoed Bolingbroke's fear that financial manipulation and political corruption had weakened the sinews of British strength. But as Isaac Kramnick argues in a major new interpretation, Burgh also anticipated nineteenth-century Protestant aversion to idleness and sloth. The recovery of virtue in Britain depended on instilling into the young the habits of hard work, a systematic pursuit of personal goals, and a personal morality, in terms reminiscent of Benjamin Franklin's admonitions in *Poor Richard's Al-*

manac. High among the virtues that Burgh praised was thoughtfulness toward other people as a recognition of human dignity: "Great people think their inferiors do only their duty in serving them and think they do theirs in rewarding their services with a nod or a smile. The lower part of mankind have minds too sordid to be capable of gratitude. It is, therefore, chiefly from the middle rank that you may look for a sense and return of kindness." Unlike Bolingbroke and other commonwealthmen, who called nostalgically for the restoration of the "ancient" British constitution as it had existed prior to Walpole and Stuart oppression, Burgh looked ahead to the day when the Crown and the House of Lords would become anachronisms and the people's representatives would rule supreme. When John Adams read that kind of prose in Burgh, he warned that, while Burgh was "excellent in some respects, and very useful," he was "extremely mistaken in the true conception of a free government," which—as will be seen in the next chapter—required distinct branches of government to check and control each other.

If James Burgh's more visionary ideas about government disturbed John Adams, the premier English radical of the Revolutionary era, Thomas Paine, alarmed him even more. Paine was a product of the radical subculture of writers, teachers, lecturers, and politically active artisans that flourished during the reign of George III. Steeped in the writings of the Commonwealth tradition, they were the vanguard of the English working-class movement, which would challenge aristocrats and early industrial employers during the turbulent generation following the French Revolution. The son of a poorly paid artisan who worshiped with Quakers, Paine excelled in science and poetry as a young man. The rationalism of science and the linguistic economy of poetry seem to have combined in Paine's discovery of a new kind of rhetoric that was spare, conversational, emotionally direct—the opposite of the ornate and florid language of the age. His first pamphlet, a 1772 appeal on behalf of underpaid excise collectors, observed that, "He who has never hunger'd may argue finely on the subjection of his appetite; and he who was never distressed may harangue as beautifully on the power of principle. But poverty, like grief, has an incurable deafness." Like the two greatest leaders of English radicalism in the 1770s, Joseph Priestley and Richard Price, Paine believed in human goodness and, like Burgh, saw no need for constitutional checks on the representatives of the people.

BURKE, A CONSERVATIVE RADICAL

One British ideological diagnosis of the origins of the American Revolution remains to be credited: Edmund Burke's moral critique of conventional Whiggery. As an Irish Protestant who had risen to eminence in British parliamentary politics, Burke combined the passionate human solidarity of the Irish with the cosmopolitan realism of the English establishment. Burke's access to power was the parliamentary faction known as the Rockingham Whigs, which rightly prided itself on its fidelity to principle, its knowledge of colonial affairs, and its defense of American liberty. Burke was the Earl of Rockingham's in-house intellectual and publicist—much as the younger Locke had been for Shaftsbury. In 1770, he wrote *Thoughts on the Cause of the Present Discontents*, a scathing attack on the venality of factional politics and a profound call for a new kind of partisanship based on shared principles, exactly what the Rockingham Whigs professed to practice. Burke believed that parliamentary supremacy extended to America, and he valued the strength of the empire. But he considered taxation of the colonies and their coercion after 1774 to be self-defeating policies that did no credit to British traditions of colonialism. "Salutary neglect," he observed in a mordant phrase, had done more to make the colonies strong and loyal to Britain than all of the attempts to enforce their legal subordination. In 1769 he prophetically told the House of Commons that "The Americans have made a discovery, or think they have made one, that we mean to oppress them; we have made a discovery, or think we have made one, that they intend to rise in rebellion. We know not how to advance; they know not how to retreat." Burke correctly perceived that resentful colonists and headstrong ministers of state were all being driven into conflict by mutual suspicions and resentments.

Conclusion: A New Bureaucratic Theory of Empire

The experts in the British imperial bureaucracy—the Treasury and, after 1767, the American Department—who had recommended, the Townshend Revenue, and the Sugar, Stamp, and Coercive acts, saw the colonists as petulant children in need of discipline from the parent state. But looking back on the situation from the vantage point of

1779, the most clear-headed of the colonial civil servants, William Knox, attributed the colonists' petulance to Britain's failure to place real political power in the hands of royal governors and to institutionalize that clout through written constitutions protecting rights and property while making colonies subject to British law. Knox believed that this structural defect made the Americans behave childishly.

Knox's lament in 1779 that Parliament had not extended British law to the colonies remained, until the recent scholarship of legal historians such as John Phillip Reid, the tip of an iceberg. Though, ostensibly, the British Constitution governed the empire, Reid and others have shown that a network of insiders in Parliament, the bureaucracy, and the legal community realized that a nascent imperial constitution had taken shape in the empire since the late seventeenth century. Most significantly, these imperial legalists agreed with colonial assemblymen that constitutional change was driven by custom rather than by the competing tugs of custom and prescription. They recognized that during the eighteenth century, the colonies had won most of the battles over precedent as the colonial assemblies circumscribed the power of Crown appointees and secured control of the purse. The critical mistake that the mother country made before the 1760s—from this perspective—had been to try to stem the outward flow of customary advantage by avoiding, or at least postponing, a direct confrontation.

The unsuccessful attempts by the Board of Trade in 1749 and 1751 to have Parliament endow the Royal Instructions to colonial governors with the rule of law were among a long series of missed opportunities to amass a counterweight of precedent supporting an invigorated royal rule. The Writs of Assistance, the Proclamation Line of 1763, the Sugar, Currency, and Stamp acts established binding precedents in the early to mid 1760s but also alerted colonial political leaders to the priceless value of their own larger store of customary liberties.

The Declaratory Act of 1766—which accompanied repeal of the Stamp Act—drew a more emphatic line with its assertion that Parliament had power to legislate for the colonies "in all cases whatsoever." In 1767 the Townshend duties generated fresh energy for an invigorated imperial rule systemically, first by establishing a precedent for taxation of colonial trade, and second by using these revenues to pay the salaries of embattled Crown appointees. The retention of the

Townshend duty on tea in 1770 seemed to provide a golden opportunity to secure an even stronger precedent if only the colonists could be induced to request repeal with a humble petition accepting the principle of the Declaratory Act, bait to which the colonies never rose.

When Rose Fisher, member of Parliament and former chief justice of Jamaica, moved repeal of the tea duty in April 1774, he exposed the ministry's high-stakes gamble of extracting from the colonies an unqualified acknowledgement of their legal subordination. "Would [the advocates of conciliation] have us surrender the right of Great Britain?" to tax its colonies, Lord Clare demanded to know. "The proposition is simply this," barrister Charles Cornwall insisted, "whether the whole of our authority over the Americans is to be taken away." Lord Beauchamp conceded that "had this repeal been proposed some sessions ago, I should probably have adopted it, but the present disturbances in America totally prevent my giving assent to it [because] we would thereby give up our right"—clearly meaning the power to tax but implying more, the power to coerce, the power to govern. Chief Justice Lord Mansfield admitted that the tea duty might be inexpedient because it kept the colonies in an uproar. "But…it [is] utterly impossible to say a syllable on the matter of expediency until the right [is] first as fully asserted on the one side as [it is] acknowledged on the other."

By denouncing the tea duty as a violation of customary liberty, American leaders had unwittingly raised the stakes in imperial politics to unprecedented heights; without meaning to do so, they had called into question the capacity of the parent state to assert its prerogatives as a metropolitan power. Legalists in the British political system appreciated that reality by 1773, and modern legal historians now confirm that the Crown was losing the battle. The Coercive Acts of 1774 and the decision to use force a year later to subdue colonial resistance were more than policy and legislative options. The empire struck back in order to establish a stronger influence over the evolution of an imperial constitution that increasingly sanctioned dangerous levels of colonial self-rule.

A British cartoon showing Virginia Whigs coercing merchants to sign the Continental Association, boycotting British trade, in 1775. *Courtesy Library of Congress.*

CHAPTER FOUR

Ideology and Character in the Revolutionary Crisis, 1774–1776

IDEOLOGIES are not disembodied systems of thought; they are expressions of the character of men and women who believe in certain values and act politically on them. Applied to revolutionaries, and for that matter to their adversaries as well, *character* denotes intellectual integrity, a structure of political and social ideas and ideals, and the ability, willingness, and even compulsion to act publicly in accordance with those beliefs.

Adams

No one illustrates better than John Adams the personal experience of internalizing an ideology. It is he who exemplifies the way the Revolutionary generation speaks to our time through the medium of writings on political history and constitutionalism. Visual impressions of Adams depict an uncomfortable man. For example, when President Washington addressed the first Senate in 1789, Vice President Adams wore a long sword that clanked noisily when he sat down, and at a dinner in France, he stammered with embarrassment when a fashionable lady teased him about his name by asking how Adam and Eve "found out the art of lying together." It is in prosaic political writing, however, that we encounter the creative, tough-minded John Adams and gain a view into the inner world of Revolutionary ideology and politics.

During the spring of 1776, colonial leaders, facing the reality that Parliament had already declared the colonies to be in a state of rebellion, began to think about writing state constitutions to legitimize the new Whig regimes that had come into being as royal administration disintegrated between the autumn of 1774 and the spring of 1775. A North Carolina delegate wrote to Adams asking his advice on how to draft a constitution. After several others asked for copies of Adams's answer, he enlarged, refined, and published it as *Thoughts on Government, Applicable to the Present State of the American Colonies in a Letter from a Gentleman to his Friend*. Widely distributed, Adams's pamphlet influenced the drafting of most of the state constitutions written in 1776 and 1777. *Thoughts on Government* is more than a manual on drafting constitutions; it is a distillation of what Adams had learned as a popular leader in Massachusetts politics during the pre-Revolutionary years, especially the crisis years of 1774 and 1775.

Recalling his own education, Adams (as is noted in Chapter Two) went to the heart of the question of what constituted legitimacy in a revolutionary regime: "In my early youth, the works of Sidney, Harrington, Lock[e], Milton, Needham, Burnet, Hoadly...convinced me that there is no good government but what is republican. The British Constitution itself is republican...[in] that it is an Empire of laws and not of men." His calling the British constitution "republican" must have startled his readers. Adams meant that the British constitutional tradition—parliamentary supremacy, the House of Commons' control of the purse, the independence of the judiciary—upheld the rule of law. That this system had been corrupted, simply confirmed the fact that constitutions were needed to curb the tendencies toward the arbitrary exercise of power that were constantly present in any government.

Such constitutional limitations ultimately depended, Adams warned, on an operative spirit or principle of government that reflected the moral character of the society it governed. The principle of a republican government was "virtue," based on the consent of the people. "Honour" might activate small states that had an aristocratic leadership, and "fear" typically buttressed governments that were controlled by force. But virtue (which, for Adams, included honor) had to be the first principle of a republican state. Adams's list of heroes—Harrington, Sidney, and Milton prominent among them—identified the republican core of his politics, and almost every line of *Thoughts on Government* echoed the humanist dream of independent and therefore virtuous property owners who were willing to share political responsibility. Their willingness to perform this duty transcended the day-to-day behavior of government officials, who in Alexander Pope's image, were "like bubbles on the sea of matter borne, they rise, they break, and to the sea return." People who had a stake in society and a tradition of public-spirited voting and officeholding were the immovable bedrock of constitutional government.

The presence of Locke's name in Adams's list alerts readers to the character of Adams's republicanism. In *Thoughts on Government*, Adams argued vigorously for a "mixed constitution," that is, one with a popularly chosen legislature, an independent executive, and an upper house that would act as a "mediator" between the other two branches of government. Adams derived this concept from Locke, and Locke, in turn, had drawn the concept of mixed government from the republican tradition and then had given it his own twist. Locke held that the legislative and executive branches of government grew out of the desire of men in a state of nature, first to preserve their lives (the basis of legislative power) and second to punish crimes against the natural law (the basis of executive power).

Adams's idea of a mediating upper house extended Locke's logic by articulating a third implicit human desire—the wish to formulate and preserve a contract between the people and the government. This was the activating principle of the upper house of the legislature. Such a branch of government could correct and offset "the fits of humour" in a popularly elected assembly, the "starts of passion, flights of enthusiasm, partialities of prejudice...productive of hasty results and absurd judgments," that public opinion generates. Likewise, the upper house would defuse conflict between the legislature and the executive, which otherwise could only end in a state of "war," in which power would be usurped by the strongest side.

For Locke, the contract inoculated the body politic against social turmoil; for Adams, Locke's discovery of the roots of the mixed constitution in the natural passions of men in a state of nature meant that ambition, desire, fear, and hope could either threaten human happiness or secure it. The key was balance. As a young man, Adams realized that "the mind must be agitated with some passion, either love, fear, or hope, before she will do her best." That Adams considered the mind a feminine entity underscored his delight in, and aversion to, sensual pleasure. Yet passion often led people astray. "We see every day," he wrote in his diary in 1772, that "our imaginations are so strong and our reason so weak, the charms of wealth and power are so enchanting, and the belief in future punishments so faint, that men find ways to persuade themselves of any absurdity, to submit to any prostitution, rather than forego their wishes and desires." Therefore, the central problem in forming a republican government was to harness human energies in the service of society—for example, to remind property owners that it was they who had the greatest stake in upholding the well-being of society. "Such is the frailty of the human heart," Adams cautioned an enthusiastic fellow patriot in 1776, "that very few men who have no property have any judgment of their own...Harrington has shown that power always follows property,...that the balance of power in a society accompanies the balance of property in land." Liberty in 1776, Adams felt, stood on knife-edge, and forming a new government could be a defining moment in which "strength, hardiness, activity, courage, fortitude, and enterprise": could come to permeate self-government. "And yet," he wrote, "I fear that human nature will be found to be the same in America as...in Europe.... They will not obtain a lasting liberty. They will only exchange tyrants for tyrannies."

Adams's influential teaching in 1776 that balancing a legislative, executive, and judicial power against each other could alone check the tendency in "human nature toward tyranny" sounds like the hallowed doctrine of separation of powers. But separation of powers was a later development in American constitutionalism—the strategy of the federal Constitution to pit powers of the President, Congress, and the judiciary against one another. What Adams championed in 1776 was the older doctrine of a "mixed constitution," in which the branches of government mirrored the structure of society, so that the political order disciplined itself in the same way that the social order preserved its coherence. Government, Adams explained, should be "an exact portrait in miniature" of society. It should "think, feel, act, and reason like the people."

Women and Revolutionary Ideology

An intimate connection between society and government delighted and troubled Adams's wife, Abigail. "Remember the ladies," and offer them protection from "the unlimited power" of their husbands, she reminded him as Congress moved toward independence. "Do not put such unlimited power in the hands of the husbands" and recognize that males are "naturally tyrannical." Under colonial law, wives were under the control of husbands, who could be "vicious" and "lawless." "If particular care and attention is not paid to the ladies, we are determined to foment a rebellion, and not hold ourselves bound by laws in which we have no voice, or representation."

Women shaped Revolutionary ideology by exerting themselves in a struggle already defined by male leadership. In support of the nonimportation boycott of British goods in 1775, a Connecticut farm girl, Betsy Foote, carded and spun ten knots of wool in one evening "and felt nationly [literally part of the nation] in the bargain." Charity Clarke, a New York City teenager, used the same phrase—that she "felt nationly" in knitting homespun stockings during the Townshend duties boycott: "Heroines may not distinguish themselves at the head of an army," but they could still contribute to the defense of liberty. Clarke could actually imagine a "new arcadia," in which "a fighting army of amazons" would confront the enemy while "men shall all learn to weave and keep sheep." Then Americans would "retire beyond the reach of arbitrary power, cloathed with the work of our own hands, and feeding on what the country affords." If men objected that women should remain in their traditional roles of wives and mothers, Mercy Otis Warren argued that they had as much at stake in the conflict as did men: "As every domestic enjoyment depends on the decision of the mighty contest, who can be an unconcerned and silent spectator? Not surely the fond mother, or the affectionate wife who trembles lest her dearest connections fall victims of lawless power or at least pour out the warm blood as a libation at the shrine of liberty." Mercy Otis Warren—sister of the patriot orator, James Otis, daughter of the Whig Patriarch, James Otis, Sr., and wife of the patriot leader, James Warren—declared that women had a unique emotional reason to interpret the Revolution ideologically as a sacrifice of innocent young men in resistance against "lawless power."

At the same time, Revolutionary ideology victimized women and raised new questions about gender and social values in the new republic. The English legal concept of "coverture," the disabilities which "a wife lie under...for her protection and benefit" (quoted in William Blackstone, *Commentaries on the Laws of England*) provided male patriots with a means of relieving women from political responsibility. This rule meant that from 1775 to 1783 married women could play no roles in the Revolution independent of their husbands, and that a male loyalist could legally compel his wife to join in his pro-British conduct. Patriot judges used the doctrine to serve another of Blackstone's doctrines—the duty of government to promote the "public good" by protecting the authority of husbands, even loyalist husbands. Courts held that allowing women to dissociate themselves from the conduct of their loyalist husbands would have negated "the most important duties of social and domestic life" and "cut asunder the bands of matrimonial union." Margaret Livingston, wife of a powerful New York patriot leader, understood that women had been politically neutralized and demeaned during the Revolutionary crisis: "You know that our sex are *doomed* to be obedient in every stage of life so that *we* shall be great losers in this contest."

Loyalist Ideology

Abigail Adams was not the only person close to John Adams whose understanding of liberty diverged from his in crucial ways. One of his closest friends, Jonathan Sewall, was the last royal Attorney General of Massachusetts. As young lawyers in the early 1760s, Adams and Sewall had spent long hours discussing the law and planning their careers. Sewall was a member of a distinguished family that had fallen on hard times. Needing powerful supporters to restore his family's prestige, Sewall chose to ally himself with the Crown and accept the label "Tory." But he advised Adams, son of a farmer, to join the political opposition because Adams had less to lose and more to gain from prominence as a Whig lawyer. Drawing on the terminology of the Exclusion controversy in England, 1679–1683, colonists crudely used the term "Whig" to identify popular opposition to British policy, "Tory" to label apologists for the British mother country. After 1776, the term "patriot" gradually replaced "Whig," and in a few years "loyalist" came to mean "Tory." Here "Whig" and "patriot" are used interchangeably, as are "Tory" and "loyalist," although as adjectives, "Whig" and "Tory" refer to the beliefs and ideas of these people, "patriot" and "loyalist" to their actions.

By the early 1770s, Adams and Sewall were leaders on opposite sides of the imperial controversy; their mutual friendship remained, but each man knew the other's strengths and weaknesses. Sewall wrote five series of anonymous newspaper articles between 1763 and 1775 refuting Whig contentions about British policy and colonial rights. In 1774 he was joined by Daniel Leonard, who, writing as *Massachusettensis* (Massachusetts man), provoked Adams into responding as *Novanglus* (New England man). (Adams felt sure that Sewall was *Massachusettensis* and did not learn until years later that Leonard had been his combatant.)

Between them, Sewall and Leonard constructed an American loyalist ideology of restraint, submission to constituted authority, obedience to British law, and aversion to what they beheld as a barbaric, unnatural, wanton rebellion. "If we look back upon the conduct of the colonies for some years past," Sewall wrote in 1775, "we...find many junctures where a prudent silence or a dutiful and rational remonstrance" would have persuaded Britain to soften the effects of taxation, trade regulation, and centralized imperial governance. Instead the Continental Congress had assumed a posture of moral rightness, poisoning the atmosphere of the empire. "Such is the unhappy frailty of human nature," he concluded, "that we are...less attentive to the calls of reason and prudence than the suggestions of passion, prejudice, and vicious habits." Adams might have agreed about passion and perhaps about prejudice, but "vicious habits" clearly referred to public demonstrations by patriots against Crown officials and attacks on their integrity, which Adams believed to be fully justified.

Governor James Wright of Georgia insisted that integrity and loyalty to the Crown were compatible. He told his Assembly in 1775, "You may be advocates for liberty. So am I, but in a constitutional and legal way.... Take heed how you give sanction to trample upon law and government, and be assured...that there can be no law without liberty. It is the due course of law and support of government which only can insure the enjoyment of your lives, liberty, and estates.... Don't catch at the shadow and lose the substance."

When Wright spoke of the substance of law and government, he meant the law as enacted by Parliament. For Whigs, like Adams, the law meant the rule of law and the subjection of law to constitutional limitations. Thus laws, such as taxes, which deprived a man of his property, fell under the constitutional doctrine of consent, and British taxes levied on colonists unconstitutionally violated the traditional power of the purse lodged by precedent in the colonial assemblies. But for the loyalists, statute law stood above constitutional law because the supremacy of Parliament—itself a constitutional doctrine vindicated by the Glorious Revolution—gave every law enacted by Parliament a constitutional justification. Even more important, statutory law was integrally bound up with the authority of the state. To question the binding validity of British statutes throughout the empire proved conclusively, Leonard asserted in the sixth *Massachusettensis* letter, that the patriots were "only one step" away from setting themselves up as "independent states."

Shaping this loyalist devotion to statute law, William Pencak argues in *War, Politics, & Revolution in Provincial Massachusetts* (1981), that it was an inductive mode of thinking that appealed to men like Sewall, Leonard, and Thomas Hutchinson, the premier Massachusetts Tory: "They observed pre-revolutionary Massachusetts and liked what they saw." Reasoning from concrete evidence led them directly to the conclusion that, as Hutchinson privately reflected, "this dispute, like all party disputes in the affairs of government,...has been carried on with great zeal and warmth of temper," and that "*this temper must subside* before there can be any room for an accommodation." What Hutchinson called "zeal and warmth" was simply Adams's conviction that the colonies stood beyond the reach of parliamentary power and owed allegiance only to the king. At the same time, Adams insisted, the colonists were obligated to resist violations of the rights of Englishmen. All of these propositions depended on deductive, rather than inductive, reasoning and proceeded from premises laid deep in British and colonial history and political practice.

To Sewall, these deductive arguments were a kind of mania. "I am far from considering the colonists...a warlike people," he wrote in a private letter in May 1775,

> but there is an enthusiasm in politics like that which religious notions inspire, that drives men on with an unnatural impetuosity that baffles and confounds all calculation based on rational principles. Liberty...is a word whose very sound carries a fascinating charm. The colonists fancy this precious jewel in danger of being ravished from them....They will not, they cannot, examine or question the truth of it until they are affrighted.

Here Sewall, at the end of his intellectual and political wits, slipped into deductive argument himself: because Whig ideology was a mass contagion, and because political experience reinforced its hold on the people, only a display of British military force—and the specter of civil war—could compel the Whigs to refrain from their treasonable course of action.

This kind of principled loyalist ideology forced the Whigs to rethink their position and recast it in more radical and elegant terms. Doing so, they seized the rhetorical high ground: the lessons of history counted far more than the immediate advantages provided by British rule. The Massachusetts Tories were beneficiaries of imperial preferment—Crown jobs, contracts, and other favors—that they took for granted. They were too apolitical to understand, much less relish, the rough and tumble of political conflict. Thus the Whigs could castigate them as greedy and privileged and eviscerate their prudent values as destructive of liberty.

Two other varieties of loyalism—one Whiggishly moderate and the other more radically conservative—entered the fray with more political sensitivity in one case and more zest in the other. The moderate loyalists rejected insistence on law and legal authority as a means of holding the empire together. "Long after the constitution [of the empire] was formed," William Smith, Jr., of New York argued, "the Empire acquired a *new, adventitious state,* and the question therefore is not what the Empire is, or was, but what, present circumstances considered, it ought to be." The key word here is "adventitious," meaning a new condition brought on by wholly new, external circumstances. Smith was a historian, a Yale graduate, a lawyer and the son of a distinguished attorney, a member of the New York Royal Council, and a leader of the Whiggish Livingston faction in provincial politics. His analysis of the nature of the empire not only envisioned the creation of an American parliament, it also examined the dynamic forces at work in North America that promised to make this continent a powerful, populous, and productive nation within a half century. The Grenville government had squandered a historic opportunity by instituting parliamentary taxation and tighter trade regulation instead of weighing the benefits to the mother country that would accrue from conciliated, happy American colonies. What Smith believed to be required during the transition from prosperous colonies in the 1760s to a powerful nation some time in the next century was a new political structure that would harmonize the interests of both parts of the empire. Legality—or what Smith called, "the constitution"—"ought to bend and *sooner* or *later* will bend, unless it is the will of heaven to...destroy us."

Smith did not publish or publicize his plan for an American parliament and his novel analysis of imperial politics, but he did send a few handwritten copies of his proposals to people in Massachusetts and in Great Britain. He hoped that highly placed political insiders would read his dramatic depiction of an empire in need of structural reform and move quietly behind the scenes to implement the necessary changes. Repeatedly in 1774 and 1775, as quotations and details from his plan kept cropping up in pamphlets and newspapers, Smith was tantalized with the hope that his ideas were "the groundwork" of a major restructuring of imperial governance.

When no such dramatic vindication materialized, Smith, in the spring of 1775, coached his Whig friends in the techniques of conciliating the British while simultaneously defending American liberties: recognize that "the present is the moment" when a major breakthrough is possible; exercise painstaking tact and diplomacy; create a moderate, dutiful opposition that the British ministry cannot divide. "Could you wish for a better opportunity to negotiate? You have the ball at your feet. For heaven's sake, don't let slip so fair a prospect." When nothing came of these behind-the-scenes maneuvers and war was inevitable, Smith returned to his diary to inscribe his thoughts for his own conduct "at this melancholy hour of approaching distress." He condemned "the pride and avarice" of British policy toward the colonies, regretted that the colonists had also neglected opportunities to achieve reconciliation, and faced the fact that the conflict would now be decided by the sword and the "omniscient judge of heaven." How that judge would rule, Smith did not presume to know, but he believed to the core of his being that war, "which would be ruinous to millions who have taken no part in the quarrel," was unconscionable: "The principle that evil may be done that good may come of it is beyond all controversy a satanical maxim."

Philadelphia was the political environment most congenial to the moderate loyalist quest for accommodation. The pluralism of its complex, prosperous social order, and the variety of opposition parties critical of the Penn family's proprietary regime, induced caution or ambivalence among much of the populace. "I can easily foresee," wrote one Philadelphia moderate, "that unnumbered calamities must burst upon these American colonies unless present difficulties between them and the parent state be speedily adjusted." The most prolific and outspoken Philadelphia moderate, the Anglican cleric and educator, William Smith—not to be confused with the New York lawyer and Councillor—urged "that the true interest of America lies in reconciliation with Great Britain upon constitutional grounds," with the British relinquishing the power to tax Americans and the colonists admitting their dependence on British power and wealth. Declaring independence or spurning reconciliation, Smith warned, would wreak havoc on Pennsylvania's web of economic interests and religious and ethnic minorities. Visionary republican schemes—"fine-spun political theories...like the quackeries of mountebank doctors"—would run afoul of the "thousand little passions and interests" of the social order. People should shrink from the "convulsion attendant upon a revolution...in government untimely attempted or finally defeated:...loss of trade,... decay of husbandry, bloodshed and desolation." The duty of the cautious moderate was complex but certain: "Let us equally shun the benumbing stillness of *overweening sloth* and the feverish activity of ill-informed zeal."

The radically conservative loyalists denounced the Revolution as religiously blasphemous, aesthetically abhorrent, philosophically bankrupt, and morally indefensible. When Congress designated July 20, 1775, as a day of prayer and fasting for the American cause, the SPG minister in Wallingford, Connecticut, the Reverend Samuel Andrews, observed the occasion with a blistering sermon on Amos 5:21: "I hate, I despise your feast days, and I will not smell of your solemn assemblies." Mocking the ritual of collective repentance as a means of mobilizing the people for revolution, Andrews warned that an "unruly," "vindictive," "ungodly spirit with those who happen to differ with us in things civil or religious" utterly destroyed the worshippers' claim to penitence. Amos expressly condemned those "*who drew near to God...while their hearts were far from him.*" The very severity of the imperial crisis, making "the clouds grow blacker and heavier," with "no sign of an accommodation...to be seen," was evidence that Americans had *not* humbled themselves sufficiently to ask for divine assistance.

Another SPG missionary in Falmouth, Massachusetts, the Reverend John Wiswall—born in New England and a Harvard graduate—had to flee the town in 1774 when his refusal to cease praying for protection from "all sedition, privy conspiracy, and rebellion" provoked the "malice and rage of a lawless rabble." Cooped up in Boston during the British occupation of the city, Wiswall saw his wife and daughter die of a violent intestinal disorder that spread through the city. Before he and his sons sailed for England in January 1776, he tried to understand "the disorder bordering on madness:" that had uprooted him, his family, and his church. Only "the God who stilleth the raging of the sea, the noise of the waves, and the *madness* of the people," he paraphrased Psalm 107, could "restore peace, order, and government to this distracted continent," because colonial society was "too free and happy" ever "to be contented with its happiness." Anticipating Jefferson's "pursuit of happiness," Wiswall used the word "happiness" to identify the painful sense of expectancy that political liberty conferred upon a people.

The New Jersey Anglican, Thomas Bradbury Chandler, went further than any other doctrinaire Tory toward defining the limitations on political liberty needed to preserve the social order. In 1774, he stipulated in *A Friendly Advice to all Reasonable Americans* that "subjects may remonstrate in a respectful manner" when governments inadvertently infringe on their rights, but they must not do so "insolently" or "rebelliously":

> The bands of society would be dissolved, the harmony of the world confounded, and the order of nature subverted, if reverence, respect, and obedience might be refused to those whom the Constitution has vested with the highest authority. *The ill-consequences of open disrespect to government are so great that no misconduct by the administration can justify or excuse it* [italics added].

Taking no prisoners in this rhetorical attack, Chandler next wrote *The American Querist...Questions...Relative to the Present Disputes*, one hundred questions designed to strip the patriot cause of any shred of intellectual respectability. For example:

> Whether Great Britain bears not a relationship to these colonies similar of that of a parent to children and whether any such parent can put up with such disrespectful and abusive treatment from children as Great Britain has recently received from her colonies? Whether in investigating the nature and causes of disorders and in fixing upon a method of cure, we ought not to have recourse to plain facts and to general and estab-

> lished principles instead of being governed by the advice...of notorious quacks and empiricks who have an interest in deceiving us?

And more fundamentally,

> Whether some degree of respect be not always due from inferiors to superiors and...whether the refusal of this...be not a violation...of the obligations of religion and morality?

Only the Maryland Anglican, Jonathan Boucher, went so far as to carry loaded pistols into the pulpit when he preached on obedience to angry Whig parishioners in July 1775. And only Boucher dared cite the notorious divine-right-of-kings theorist Robert Filmer—at least in the version of the sermon published in England in 1797—to support the view that "kings and princes" derived their authority "from God, the source and origin of all power," rather than from any "supposed consent...of men." But Boucher and other doctrinaire loyalists were much more forward-looking and constructive when they criticized the patriots' concept of liberty. "Liberty," Boucher argued,

> is not the setting at naught and despising established laws [note the reference to statutes], much less making our own wills the rule of our own actions,...but it is to be governed by the law and the law only....To pursue liberty in any way not warranted by law, [meaning British statutes] whatever the pretext may be, is clearly hostile to liberty.

When patriot mobs enforcing the nonimportation boycott on British goods began to search Tory houses without legal authority and threatened and abused those who stood in their way, one New York loyalist asked pointedly: "Is this the liberty we seek?"—liberty to deny the rights of a loyal subjects, liberty to descend into barbarous conduct?

Pennsylvania Radicalism

When John Adams recommended constitutional limitations on the power of Revolutionary legislatures, he sought to insure that the loyalist nightmare did not become reality, that the Revolution did not degenerate into licentiousness. Only one state, Pennsylvania, rejected Adams's brand of constitutionalism. "We are determined not to pay the least regard to the former constitution of this province," one Pennsylvania radical boasted, "but to reject everything therein....We are resolved to clear every part of the old rubbish out of the way and begin upon a clean foundation." By the "former constitution," he meant the proprietary rule of the Penn family under the charter from the Crown.

The Revolutionary movement in Pennsylvania sought to obliterate four older political alignments: (1) the proprietary family, (2) the dominant antiproprietary party organized by Benjamin Franklin and led in the 1770s by Joseph Galloway, (3) the Whiggish opposition to Galloway and to British colonial policy led by John Dickinson and James Wilson, and (4) the sizable Quaker and German minorities in the province. Though Dickinson (author of the *Letters of a Pennsylvania Farmer*, see Chapter One) and Wilson (a lawyer educated in Scotland) were strongly republican in their ideology, their awareness of Pennsylvania's political fragility made them reluctant to decalare independence from Britain in 1776. Into that vacuum came the radicals whom Gordon S. Wood, in *The Creation of the American Republic, 1776–1787*, calls "new men,...James Cannon, Timothy Matlack, Robert Whitehill, George Bryan—all socially outside the establishment (Matlack, it was said, 'does not keep a chariot') and hardly known in Pennsylvania,...who sought...to pick up the pieces of political power." Benjamin Rush, an early supporter of these men who later turned against them out of disagreement with their radical constitutional ideas, remembered vividly his introduction to the republicanism of Algernon Sidney. A Scottish friend of Rush's, whose ancestors had supported Cromwell, had once visited the country house in which Sidney had "composed his famous treatise on government.... He spoke [to Rush] in rapture of the character of Sidney.... Never before had I heard the authority of Kings called in question." Rush encouraged the visiting English radical, Thomas Paine, to publish his electrifying pamphlet, *Common Sense* (1776), which demanded independence on the ground that monarchy was corrupt and that the people in their purity and virtue should construct a new government spontaneously. The radicals persuaded Congress to call on all thirteen colonies to institute governments based on the consent of the governed, a standard that the proprietary regime could not meet. A mass meeting in May 1776 called for a constitutional convention, which, during that summer, drafted a document providing for a unicameral legislature, a weak executive and judiciary, a periodic Council of Revision to correct violations of the Constitution, the publication of laws in advance of their enactment, and voting to be enjoyed by all taxpayers rather than, as in other states, most property owners. This provision swept away, in J. R. Pole's words, "the basic...presumption that ownership of a specified amount of property was an essential guarantee of political competence." "Good God," reacted a shocked John Adams—who had initially supported the radicals—"the people of Pennsylvania in two years will be glad to petition...Britain for reconciliation in order to be delivered from the tyranny of their Constitution."

Adams had overreacted, as he often did when people ignored his views on libertarian theory. Pennsylvania did not succumb to the tyranny of the majority under its 1776 constitution, though the new government treated pacifists and neutralists harshly. The radical quality of the Pennsylvania Constitution of 1776 was that it excluded from power for nearly fifteen years many moderate Whigs and instead ensconced power in newcomers to Philadelphia—men more likely to be Scots-Irish and evangelical than English and religiously traditional.

What was revolutionary about Pennsylvania politics in 1776 was the recognition that society consisted of people rather than social orders. Republicanism made the independent landowner a member of a social group with a shared capacity for virtue, and it recognized a legitimate tension between the concerns of farmers, merchants, and aristocrats. Adams had sought to balance numbers against wealth with a bicameral legislature. The Pennsylvania radicals rejected that approach in favor of "a large, equal, and annual representation in one house *only* [in which] the different parties, by being blended together, would hear each other's arguments, which advantage they cannot have if they sit in different houses. To say there ought to be two houses because there are two sorts of interest is the very reason there ought to be one, and *that one* to consist of every sort." This was revolutionary, but not because it was socially leveling; the Pennsylvania radicals were middle-class men on the make who yearned for riches. It was revolutionary in the sense that it caught a vision of the future of American politics in which democratic government would bring together leaders from several strata of society and compel them to take each other seriously.

Conclusion: Price, Jefferson, and the Meaning of Liberty

The supreme challenge for statesmen and libertarians on both sides of the Atlantic was to break through the impasse between the past and the future—between imperial sovereignty over the colonies and secure guarantees of American liberty. Several attempts—some more short-sighted than others—had been made. First, the Coercive Acts had sought to stun the colonists into submission as a necessary precondition for restoring tranquillity and preserving as much colonial autonomy as was consistent with the maintenance of the empire. Then the first Continental Congress's "Declaration of Rights and Grievances" demanded a return to 1763—a repudiation of all laws and measures restricting the colonies since the end of the last war with France. In the aftermath of British military action at Lexington and Concord in April 1775, Congress issued its "Declaration Justifying the Taking Up of Arms." It insisted that the Continental army was defensive only and not an assault on British sovereign power. The king and Parliament both responded by declaring the colonies to be in a state of rebellion, though Lord North kept the door open for individual colonies to return to obedience. The writing of state constitutions, which began in the spring of 1776 (before independence), was initially an effort to stabilize provisional rebellious regimes rather than to create a fully independent nation. Each nudge closer to an unknown future drew upon various Anglo-American ideological resources, upon people's deepest understandings of history and morality.

Richard Price made the English radical case for American liberty in his *Observations on the Nature of Civil Liberty, the Principles of Government, and the Justice and Polity of the War with America* (1776). The rationalist Enlightenment taught Price that liberty was an absolute right of mankind, that people surrendered none of their natural freedom when they entered the compact with government. The only restriction on human freedom then was the natural impossibility of everyone acting simultaneously as he or she wished. As people in a particular nation or "kingdom" accommodated themselves to others' needs to act freely, they established a practical level of liberty for themselves and everyone else. In an "empire," each colony enjoyed the same freedom to act as long as its actions did not harm other parts of the empire. But here again, resolution of conflict had to result from voluntary action rather than from imposed authority. Price had broken through to a moral theory of empire that was incomprehensible to British officialdom.

Thomas Jefferson was the American who moved most decisively toward a libertarian future, and, like Price, he found the key in ethics rather than in law or public policy. Jefferson spent the decade between attending college at William and Mary and his marriage in 1772 as a law student and then as a bookish bachelor devouring the works of the Enlightenment, English history and law, and the classics. He also received his political education in the House of Burgesses. Like his counterpart in Massachusetts, John Adams, Jefferson absorbed the republicanism of the English country party and the Scottish moralists as well as the empiricism and natural-rights philosophy of Locke. Jefferson's ability to move back and forth between these two sources of insight made him an adroit leader in the crises of 1774–1776.

On the eve of the Revolutionary crisis, Jefferson brooded over the English law of treason, and he brooded over death. He took copious notes on the use of treason as a tool of statecraft in medieval and Stuart England, and he transcribed passages about death from ancient and modern writers, including Herodotus, Cicero, Milton, Shakespeare, and Pope, who depicted death in a just cause as obedience to God. Then, in 1774, he devoted himself to drafting a historical explanation of the imperial-colonial controversy, *A Summary View of the Rights of British North America*. Drawing on early eighteenth-century commonwealth writers, especially the exiled Huguenot historian, Paul Rapin, Jefferson fastened upon the plausible myth of an ancient Saxon constitution prior to the Norman conquest of 1066. It allegedly granted subjects rights of participation in the king's government and made land tenure a matter of common deliberation rather than of royal edict. In this version of English history, feudalism was the work of Norman kings and their cunning lawyers.

Jefferson urged Americans to demand the restoration of ancient Saxon liberty. By so doing, they would affirm that the colonies and the British Isles were distinct, equal, and coordinate branches of the empire: "Let no act be passed by any one legislature [in the empire] which may infringe on the rights and liberties of another. This is the important post in which fortune has placed you, holding the balance of a great, if well poised, Empire." Jefferson's claim that no legislature in the empire could infringe on any other legislature was exactly Richard Price's point. Jefferson's view that the cause of liberty had passed from English libertarian heroes into American hands echoed contemporary British opposition thinkers such as Francis Hutcheson and James Burgh.

Within two years, the whole effort to renounce the authority of Parliament and yet preserve the colonies' place in the empire collapsed. The eloquence and powerful historical imagination of *A Summary View* made Jefferson the obvious choice to draft Congress' Declaration of Independence in late June 1776. Here Jefferson jettisoned the Saxon myth as his historical framework and moral reference point and in its place put Locke's theory of natural rights as guaranteed by an implicit contract and ultimately protected by the right of revolution.

From Garrett Ward Sheldon's textual comparison of Locke and Jefferson in *The Political Philosophy of Thomas Jefferson* (1991), we know that Jefferson's fidelity to Locke and his modifications of Locke are both important. "We hold these truths to be self-evident ["sacred & undeniable" in Jefferson's first draft] that all men are created equal"; "equal and independent" in Jefferson's first draft echoed Locke's view that "all men are by nature equal." Like Locke's belief that "every man hath...equal right...to his natural freedom," Jefferson held that "from that equal creation they derive rights inherent and inalienable," which the finished document ascribed to "their Creator." On the crucial matter of the hypothetical contract, Locke has "man...joyn in society with others...for the mutual preservation of their lives, liberties, and estate." Jefferson wrote: "to secure these ends, governments are instituted among men." Both Locke and Jefferson used the phrase "long train of abuses" as grounds for a revolution, but for Jefferson revolution meant to "throw off such government and provide new guards for...future security," while Locke ruminated thoughtfully that "tis not to be wondered that they should then rouze themselves...to put the rule into such hands which may secure to them the ends for which government was first erected."

The most striking Jeffersonian modification of Locke was his substitution of "pursuit of happiness" for "property" as a natural right. Locke, to be sure, defended man's "uncontrolled enjoyment" of his natural rights—language close to the idea of pursuing happiness by holding property and living in legal security. But as Forrest McDonald and Garrett Sheldon argue, Jefferson must have derived that concept from Aristotle, who wrote that men promote the public good as a means of attaining, what "cultivated men...call, happiness."

Jefferson spent a half century pondering the drafting of the Declaration—he and John Adams died fifty years to the day after July 4, 1776. Only ten days before his death, Jefferson bequeathed to his countrymen and to posterity his mature interpretation of what the Declaration meant. For the celebration at the Capitol, he prepared a message that read in part: "The mass of mankind has not been born with saddles on their backs nor a favored few booted and spurred to ride them." That arresting metaphor paraphrased closely the speech that Colonel Richard Rumdold delivered from his gallows in Edinburgh before he was beheaded, drawn, and quartered for his alleged role in a conspiracy to kill Charles II in 1683—the same trumped-up charge that cost Algernon Sidney his life. (Rumdold had said that "none comes into the world with a saddle on his back, neither any boot'd or spurr'd to ride him.") Jefferson probably had those words—and Rumdold's gruesome death—in mind while in Philadelphia in late June and early July 1776, for there were in his library at that time three books containing that story, one by Paul Rapin, one by Gilbert Burnet, and one by James Burgh—each book a classic of radical Whig belief.

America Triumphant and Britannia in Distress, from *Weatherwise's Town and Country Almanack* (1782). *Courtesy Library of Congress.*

CHAPTER FIVE

Revolutionary War and the Sources of Conflict in American Society, 1776–1783

THE War for Independence was preeminently a war of ideas—a clash of ideologies. Britain's decision in 1775 to crush the rebellion with force was, at the most elemental level, a parental rebuke of a disobedient, willful, and ungovernable child. In a larger sense, it signified the British nation's duty and right, as a metropolitan center of commerce, culture, and authority, to radiate order outward to the far-flung peripheries of its empire.

The patriots' appeal to arms rested both on the Lockean right of a free people "to levy war, conclude peace, contract alliances...and do all acts and things which independent states may of right do," and on the republican conviction that the king and his ministers had become ravenous and brutish.

There were thus two British justifications for military action, and two American reasons for the appeal to arms. Exploring the conflicts *within* the British—and *within* the American—conceptions of the war is a first step in understanding the ideas at stake in the conflict.

Two British military strategies warred for supremacy within the councils of the empire during the first two years of the war. Led by Colonial Secretary George Germain and supported by King George III himself, a small core of hawkish officials believed that an overwhelming exertion of military force would defeat and humiliate the rebellious colonists and thus lay the groundwork for restoring obedience and tranquility. Skeptical of Germain's faith in the efficacy of retribution was a larger and more amorphous group led by Lord North, which included General William Howe and his brother, Admiral Richard Howe, named respectively in 1775 to command the British army and naval forces in America. They believed that the passions and costs of war on both sides of the Atlantic would disrupt society and make the eventual reconciliation more difficult. The brothers Howe therefore planned military operations that would be limited to securing specific political objectives and minimize bloodshed.

From July 1776 until September 1778, both Germain and the Howes independently pursued their separate agendas. Germain mobilized the 20,000-man British and Hessian force that assembled on Staten Island in 1776. Germain planned General John Burgoyne's 1777 march, from Quebec toward a rendezvous with Col. Barry St. Leger near Albany, which ended in disaster when Burgoyne was forced to surrender at Saratoga to the American general, Horatio Gates. In the meantime, Howe had occupied New York City, northern New Jersey, and the port city of Newport, Rhode Island, in the autumn of 1776, and then spent all of the next spring and summer moving his forces by sea to the northern tip of Chesapeake Bay and then into Philadelphia by late September 1777—too late to move northward, up the Hudson River to support Burgoyne, as Germain had intended. The consequences of Howe's mistiming were important, for Saratoga emboldened France to enter the war in early 1778, forcing Britain for the first time to make hard choices about the kind of war it wanted to wage in America.

The Americans, too, had a hard choice to make between fighting a war in accordance with European military etiquette or employing a more violent and unpredictable style of warfare as practiced on the American frontier. General Charles Lee—a professional soldier from England who had emigrated to New York in 1773 and volunteered for service in the American army in 1775—proposed some time in early 1778 to decentralize American armed resistance and to depend instead on small, autonomous bands of conscripts to harry the British army and render the American states unconquerable: "Harassing and impeding can alone succeed!" The whole idea was an attack on Washington's determination to make the Continental army a disciplined, respectable European-style fighting force.

These disagreements within the British and within the American high commands cast in high relief the competing values of British and American society. Germain believed in a *retribution* inflicted by imperial authority on provincial rebels. The Howes held a *metropolitan* world view, in which centers of civilized authority appropriately governed far-flung colonial possessions. Washington admired the gentility of European commanders as well as the classical standards of *moderation.* He intended to discipline the patriots' appeal to arms by observing both moderate and refined standards of behavior. Lee realized that a *radical*, irregular war, even if it sacrificed both gentility and moderation in American conduct, would be the kind of conflict that Britain could not win.

British *retribution* and *metropolitanism* and American *moderation* and *radicalism* continued to interact throughout the War for Independence, because warfare is both armed struggle and symbolic behavior. The connection between armed violence and symbolic (or psychological) force is best understood in the American Revolutionary setting from historian John Shy's widely accepted portrayal of the Revolutionary War as a "triangular" conflict. Shy suggests that the British and Continental armies and respective Tory provincial corps and state militia allies all sought to overawe elements of a large apolitical mass of the American population in order to recruit neutrals to one side or the other and deny the enemy the manpower and supplies necessary to secure territorial control. If outright defeat of the enemy's main force eluded the British and was never a possibility for the Americans, gaining the grudging respect of perhaps half of the population that was not yet committed to either side could be decisive.

Thus battles, campaigns, the occupations of towns and their surrounding countryside, the treatment of prisoners of war and noncombatants, the collection of supplies, the improvising of military finance, the conducting of relations with French or Indian allies, and the use made of militia and irregular volunteers all projected strong signals to those people who, leery of backing a loser, wondered which side might prevail. The aura as well as the reality of military power was just as strong an ideological force as pamphlets and oratory. "Ye brave, honest subjects who dare to be loyal," in the popular loyalist song, "The Rebels," expressed the Tory and British view of the utter abnormality of the American rebellion:

> Come listen awhile, and I'll sing you a song,
> I'll show you those Yankees are all in the wrong,
> Who with blustering look and a most awkward gait,
> 'Gainst their lawful Sov'reign dare for to prate,
> With their hunting shirts and rifle guns,...
> With their hunting shirts and rifle guns.

Retribution

Germain's determination to use force to crush "rebellious resistance" aggravated severe ethnic, racial, and social tensions in America. And Germain and other imperial officials in America tried to exploit these tensions to Britain's advantage. In November 1775, Lord Dunmore, governor of Virginia, promised slaves who deserted patriot masters to fight for the Crown that they would be freed in reward. The following January, Governor Josiah Martin of North Carolina sent word to the Highland Scots in the upper Cape Fear valley that they should join other backcountry loyalists who were then marching on Wilmington, North Carolina, to rendezvous with a British force headed there by sea. In northern New Jersey, the loyalist Daniel Isaac Brown exploited a bitter religious feud within the Dutch Reformed Church by appealing to Dutch traditionalists to support the Crown and stigmatized the Americanized branch of the church as a collection of libertine anarchists. When the British army occupied the Hackensack Valley in October 1776, Brown's Dutch recruits made up a substantial part of the 30 percent of the Jersey population that openly sided with the British. In the Mohawk Valley of New York, the Mohawk leaders Joseph Brant and his sister, Mary Brant, offered to recruit an elite Mohawk military force to secure the New York frontier for the British; on the Georgia frontier, the Creek leader Alexander McGillivray organized a similar Indian force in 1777.

As a part of Governor James Wright's policy in Georgia during the early 1770s to settle the interior, he had negotiated a vast cession of Cherokee lands. In return, the Cherokees secured liquidation of large debts to British creditors and a strategic position in future commerce with British and colonial suppliers. Another beneficiary was a Yorkshireman named Thomas Brown, who secured a large land grant on which he constructed a handsome country house in 1774. Confronted on his own front porch in August 1775 by a crowd of armed Whigs who demanded his support for the trade boycott against Britain, Brown had his skull fractured from a blow with a rifle butt and the soles of his feet punctured with burning splinters. Brown fled to St. Augustine, in East Florida, where he spent the early years of the war organizing other dispossessed loyalists into a ferocious military force called the East Florida Rangers.

None of these initiatives by Crown officials or their colonial supporters succeeded in strangling the patriots' military resistance in its cradle. Brown did, however, remain a formidable loyalist military leader throughout the war. The 800 Virginia slaves who made their way to Norfolk in response to Dunmore's proclamation left the Chesapeake in August 1776, and most of them died of shipboard diseases. The defeat of the Highland Scots loyalists at Moore's Creek in February 1776 by a Whig militia eliminated the loyalists as a military threat in North Carolina until Cornwallis's invasion of the state in 1781. After Washington's victories at Trenton and Princeton at the beginning of 1777, Howe's forces pulled out of northern New Jersey, leaving the loyalists to come to terms with their patriot neighbors. White loyalists on the New York frontier at first denied Joseph Brant command over Indian warriors and then failed to feed those Indians whom they had recruited. Not until 1778 did Brant get a chance to fight in his own way, and then the Continental army effectively eliminated the Indian threat by burning Mohawk villages and crops. Similar confusion and violence prevented McGillivray's Creeks and other southern tribes from adding strength to British forces on the Georgia and South Carolina frontiers.

These British and loyalist efforts to fracture the unity of Revolutionary America along ethnic, racial, and social lines were a natural consequence of Germain's policy of retributive warfare. The conflicts reflected and intensified ideologies of outsider groups in American society. Ethnic communities apprehensive about the attitudes of the English-stock majority reacted to the Revolution by speeding their assimilation into the dominant culture. On the other hand, frontier loyalists, both Indian and British, became, after 1783, British, French, and Spanish operatives in the Mississippi Valley and Great Lakes region and intended to play a historic role in thwarting American manifest destiny. As it turned out, the Napoleonic Wars forced the European powers to withdraw manpower and money from the North

American interior between 1803 and 1807. But, as will be seen, African Americans and Native Americans brought to the Revolution their own concepts of justice and power; these values, in turn, became a part of the ideological character of the War for Independence because white Americans responded to racial militancy with a self-protective ideology of their own.

NATIVE AMERICANS

The outbreak of the War for Independence pressured Indian tribes to side with either the British or the Americans for self-defensive reasons, or to opt for the more difficult course of defending their neutrality against depredations from both sides. These difficult choices were surface manifestations of a deeper struggle within Indian culture—a culture reverberating since the 1730s with waves of religious prophecy. The prophets had proclaimed two different spiritual messages. One affirmed pan-Indian power as the appropriate response to the intrusion of the whites. The other appealed for accommodation with the whites as a way of holding the intruders at bay.

Pan-Indian and accommodationist spirituality both depended on ritual. As Gregory Evans Dowd explains in *A Spiritual Resistance: The North American Indian Struggle for Unity, 1745–1815* (1992), "ritual loomed large...because ritual delivered the assistance of sacred powers" and access to "the upper world," where abundant sources of power lay waiting to be claimed by those who knew the secret of spiritual empowerment.

Indian accommodationist beliefs mixed doctrines of spiritual power with Christian concepts learned from missionaries. David Zeisberger, the Moravian missionary to Indians north of the Ohio River, attributed the Indian converts' interest in Christianity to their need for allies, including the Christians' God, as they jockeyed for position with other Indian tribes. The Delaware leader, White Eyes, saw Indian and white religion as complementary. Quakers and missionaries, he declared, "were brought up together [in Pennsylvania]; it is our Saviour's mind that they should be of one religion."

Both the pan-Indians and the accommodationists knew that basing their politics on sacred principles entailed risks. "Old Tassell," the pan-Indian Cherokee leader, whose murder by whites in 1788 would unite all Cherokees in armed retaliation, had in 1777 defied American demands for land cessions in return for schools and missions. "The Great Spirit," he declared, "has given you many advantages, but he has not created us to be your slaves. We are a separate people." Likewise the Wyandot accommodationist and pro-British leader, Pomoacan, knew in 1781 that welcoming Moravian missionaries to tribal towns placed his people in spiritual as well as military danger: "Two powerful and mighty gods are standing and opening wide their jaws toward each other…," he told the Wyandot, Delaware, Shawnee, Ottawa, and Chippewa Indians living around a Moravian mission in the Ohio Territory, "and between the two angry spirits, who thus open their jaws, you are placed." Pacifists though the Moravians were, the British commanders and loyalists in the region may have suspected the truth that even the missionary, David Zeisberger, supplied military intelligence to the patriots.

But Pomoacan's imagery about "jaws" and "ravenous spirits" was more than a metaphor. The Revolution compelled British and American forces to intrude deep into Wyandot life. This intrusion made accommodation a necessary evil; at the same time it involved Indians in flirtation with the "snake," or male tempter. In Shawnee belief, the snake stood in opposition to the superior—and feminine—source of power, menstrual fluid, which was the embodiment of life and regeneration. Here the serpent, with its phallic symbolism, was both male and political—accommodation was a masculine form of confronting the white enemy—while women's menstrual fluids symbolized a purer and more radical response to danger. The Shawnees employed these symbols to prophesy the final triumph of a radical and feminine truth over an accommodationist and masculine understanding of politics.

Though oblivious to the details of Indian spirituality and politics, the leaders of the American Revolution sensed the broad outlines of this Indian strategy: militant resistance modified by shrewd negotiation. They filled in the gaps with speculations drawn from their Enlightenment rationalism. To Jefferson and his kind, Indians occupied a position below whites but above that of African slaves; and unlike Africans, who were deemed incapable of forming a civilization, Indians had the virtues of bravery and an understanding of nature that made them susceptible to becoming yeoman farmers. If they would shed their own culture and till the soil and live in peace, Jefferson felt sure that there was a place for Indians in the new republic.

AFRICAN AMERICANS

Slavery and the fear of slave insurrection presented the British with another weakness in American society to be exploited militarily. As the response to Dunmore's proclamation revealed, the entire colonial South was seething with African-American hunger for freedom. Throughout the Chesapeake, Whigs in Maryland and Virginia caught bands of blacks far from their home plantations who were apparently trying to reach Dunmore's base at Norfolk. In Charleston, South Carolina, in May 1775, a free black ship pilot, Thomas Jeremiah, told another black man that the conflict between Britain and the colonies could prove a "help to the poor Negroes" and that for the war that seemed imminent, blacks like himself were collecting gun powder and arms. Allegedly, Jeremiah assigned himself the "chief command of the said Negroes." Over the strenuous objections of the now powerless royal governor, South Carolina Whigs hanged and burned Jeremiah as an example to any slave who might take advantage of the Revolution.

As Jeremiah's analysis of the Revolution suggests, black militancy was based on an astute understanding of the nature of power and of morality—and thus it was ideological in the same sense as Jefferson's fusion of politics and morality. In 1800, Gabriel Prosser, a slave coachman, organized a large-scale armed black uprising near Richmond, Virginia, which was suppressed when one of the conspirators prematurely revealed Prosser's plans. Just before one of Gabriel's men was sentenced to hang, a judge asked routinely if he had anything to say. "I have nothing more to offer," the man replied, "than what General Washington would have to offer had he been taken by the British officers and put to trial by them: 'I have ventured my life in endeavoring to obtain the liberty of my countrymen and am a willing sacrifice to their cause.'" There are indications that Thomas Jeremiah and this nameless participant in Prosser's conspiracy were not isolated examples of African-American militancy during the age of the American Revolution. Both David Walker, a former slave in North Carolina who wrote an important abolitionist tract, *Appeal to the Coloured Citizens of the World* (1829), and Denmark Vesey, a free black carpenter in Charleston, South Carolina, who organized an abortive black uprising in 1822, had attended black evangelical churches for much of their lives and constructed from biblical and historical sources an ideology of black liberation.

Just as the political maturity of the Indians left a mark on the politics of white Americans in the post–Revolutionary period, so did African-American militancy spread fear and loathing among many white Americans—and for some it affected their idealism and political courage. Much of what we do know about the ideology of African Americans in the Revolution comes to us reflected through whites who either despised or respected black assertions of human dignity.

In 1778, John Laurens of South Carolina, a brilliant and charismatic officer in the Continental army, proposed to his father, Henry Laurens, that the patriots should arm their slaves to fight against the British and then emancipate those who did so. This was not the first time a South Carolinian had proposed arming slaves in wartime, but as the historian Robert M. Weir explains, the "astonishing" quality of John Laurens's proposal was "its candor, its boldness, and its larger purpose": "We have sunk the African and their descendants below the standard of humanity" by unjustly depriving them of "the rights of mankind." Laurens envisioned service in the Continental army as a way-station, "a proper gradation between abject slavery and perfect freedom....I have long deplored the wretched state of these men,... the bloody wars excited in Africa to furnish America with slaves, the groans of despairing multitudes toiling for the luxuries of merciless tyrants." When Laurens returned to South Carolina to campaign for this gradual emancipation, the planter-merchant aristocracy responded with what Laurens called "prejudice, avarice, and pusillanimity." Deeply shaken by their failure to appreciate his libertarian motives and the "moral beauty" of his proposal, Laurens plunged recklessly into the campaign to drive the British from South Carolina. He died in one of the last skirmishes of the war.

More than any other patriot, Jefferson squirmed uncomfortably in his disparate roles as the conscience of the Revolution and the owner of slaves. He supported a 1782 Virginia statute simplifying manumission, and he hoped that slavery would die a natural death. In his *Notes on Virginia* (1784), he lamented that slavery blighted the moral sense of white children who, at an impressionable age, saw their fellow human beings treated with casual cruelty "and thus nursed, educated, and exercised in tyranny, cannot but be stamped by it with odious peculiarities."

The same nagging questions prompted Jefferson's young neighbor, Edward Coles, twenty-two years later, to invite Jefferson to lead a public crusade in Virginia on behalf of emancipation. Jefferson replied to Coles that he still considered slavery a moral blight on Virginia society, but that he was now too old and exhausted by the political wars to take a public stand on so explosive an issue; "I had always hoped," he told Coles, "that the younger generation, receiving their early impressions after the flame of liberty had been kindled in every breast, and had become, as it were, the vital spirit of every American,...would have sympathized with [those under] oppression wherever found and proved their love of liberty beyond their share of it." Jefferson's reply to Coles was not as evasive as it sounds. The historian William W. Freehling defends Jefferson's cautious approach to slavery, pointing out that by excluding slavery from the Northwest Territory in 1787 and ending the importation of slaves in 1808, Jefferson and his supporters made a preemptive strike on slavery that prevented the institution from aggressively expanding in the 1850s. Herein lay the crux of the influence of race on Revolutionary ideology: the equality proclaimed by the Declaration of Independence was a responsibility the founders decided to share with future generations, an ethical mortgage entailed by one generation but decades—perhaps centuries—away from full repayment.

Metropolitanism

The metropolitan professionalism of British commanders did not evoke the kinds of widespread conflict that Germain's retributive war policy spawned, but metropolitanism was just as ideological an outlook as Germain's. Metropolitanism was an attitude reflecting Britain's responsibility and duty to radiate power outward from London to the far-flung colonial outposts of British civilization; metropolitan political values dictated a military response to colonial rebellion that balanced goals against risks, kept Britain's overall foreign policy interests in mind, and exhibited patience and persistence in bringing the American rebels back to subordination. While Generals Gage, Howe, Clinton, Cornwallis, and Carleton (governor in Quebec who succeeded Clinton in 1782), had disagreements and differences over tactics and military administration, they shared metropolitan values.

As military professionals, they reflected the effort under George III to promote officers based on merit rather than social standing in a society riddled with patronage and favoritism. This professionalization of the military dramatized the metropolitan understanding of national power and the capacity of figures like the king, who took a personal interest in the army, to bend institutions to meet the military requirements of great-power status. But as military professionals, British commanders in America still had to work within a political system ill-equipped to make hard, rational choices. Shortly after Gage became royal governor of Massachusetts, he reported to the ministry that enforcement of the Coercive Acts was proceeding smoothly. Then, as is noted in Chapter One, massive demonstrations and a threat of violence forced the appointees to the new Royal Council to flee their homes and seek refuge in Boston, where Gage commanded British troops. Gage calmly informed London that he had lost control of the Massachusetts countryside and that all of New England had joined the insurgency. Nothing more could be done until a much larger British and German mercenary force could be sent to the region. The ministry was incredulous. Blaming Gage for failing to take firm action, the government decided that he must be replaced. In fact, Gage's assessment of the situation, and his prudent use of the forces at his disposal, were models of military realism and effective command.

His successors each showed comparable coolness and skill. Howe occupied New York City in September 1776 and Philadelphia a year later with a minimum of bloodshed; as governor of Quebec, Carleton worked closely with experienced British Indian agents to prevent indiscriminate Indian attacks against white patriots, as did Colonel Alexander Prevost in East Florida. Cornwallis's defeat of Horatio Gates at the Battle of Camden in August 1780 was a masterpiece of conventional battlefield command, and his pursuit of Nathanael Greene from Charlotte, North Carolina, to the Dan River in Virginia the following winter, though unsuccessful, was a bold adaptation to the new frontier war he found himself fighting. Henry Clinton understood better than anyone else the connection between sea power and land movements; he skillfully kept the French fleet drawn away from North American waters during the southern offensive of 1778–1781 until the French admiral, the Comte de Grasse, entered Chesapeake Bay in force in September 1781, cutting off Cornwallis from reinforcements and forcing his surrender. If war is symbolic action that seeks to overawe and impress the enemy through the intelligent application of force, the metropolitan professionalism of British commanders was surely an expression of the character of the British nation and one of the strongest features of its political system.

Closely related to their professionalism was the political sagacity of British commanders. For Howe, war was an extension of the politics of subordination—yet another way of persuading the rebellious colonists that their appeal to arms would not bring them liberty or happiness. As commander of the garrison town of New York, Clinton courageously resisted loyalist demands for the use of terror—kidnapping patriot leaders and treating political prisoners with cruelty. The vengeful garrison-town loyalists finally went over Clinton's head to get authorization for covert, civilian, counterrevolutionary action, but Clinton's skepticism and resistance to this whole idea reflected his superior understanding of the nature of the patriot regime that he was fighting. When Carleton, in 1782, took command of British forces in the aftermath of Yorktown, he shrewdly noted that the patriots did not have the resources or the will to eject the British garrison from New York by force. Carleton immediately urged the caretaker ministry in London to refuse to budge from New York until the Americans conceded some symbolic tie to the Crown. Had Carleton been supported by the ministry in London, this strategy would have caused the exhausted American regime enormous political and military problems. The momentary paralysis of British will in 1782 saved the new republic from a severe test.

The metropolitan values of the British commanders operated in the empire because they stabilized a system in which power necessarily radiated from the imperial center to the colonial periphery. What was clear and direct in London could be ambiguous and slippery 3,000 miles away. Metropolitanism was an ideology that sought to civilize and rationalize the exertion of central authority in peripheral settings; in professionally competent, politically astute commanders of British forces in North America, Britain transported to the scene of action some of the stability and mastery of the metropolitan center.

Moderation

Just as British commanders were sophisticated men of the world, the highest level of American military command—members of the Continental Congress and the commander of its army, George Washington—were men who had learned from history and personal experience that the world is a dangerous place and that caution, prudence, and carefully planned and skillfully executed acts of boldness are essential to survival. The term that encompasses these attitudes, moderation, is easily misunderstood. It means much more than the mere avoidance of extremes. "Moderation" is one of three conceptions of *the self* that Philip Greven explored in *The Protestant Temperament* (1977). (His other two categories are "evangelical," the conviction that the self is evil and must be suppressed, and "genteel," the outlook of people with enough refinement to regard the self as deserving to be asserted.) Greven's moderates and their commitment to the control of the self became the norm for American society and particularly for its political leadership and constitutional government. The War for Independence tested and strongly reinforced moderation as a personal creed and societal value.

THE CLASSICS

Moderation was a republican virtue drawn from classical Roman sources. But as a means of combating sinful human nature, it was also a Protestant value, and as a disciplined way of upholding the compact it was a Lockean value as well. During the War for Independence, Revolutionary ideology oscillated between a Protestant view of moderation, which stressed the need for fortitude in the long struggle, and the republican conviction that without discipline, all could be lost. In May 1777, with Howe's army moving against Philadelphia and Washington's army untested in the field, John Adams turned to classical republicanism for guidance. He carefully reread Plutarch's life of Sulla and Sallust's account of the turmoil of the last decades of the Roman republic. Sulla was the Roman general who imposed order—and sought to restore Roman republic virtue—in 83 to 79 B.C., a generation before Julius Caesar. In a fierce civil war between rival generals, Sulla, Marius, and Lucius Scipio, the armies that Sulla and his rivals headed were motley collections of Roman and other Italian soldiers whose allegiance their generals bought with the prospect of booty. Adams believed that treachery toward rivals was also a key feature of Sulla's character. He cited Sulla's attempt to lure his rival, Fimbria, into an alliance, Sulla's subsequent betrayal of Fimbria, and Fimbria's suicide, as an example of how politically manipulative generals operate. "Howe is no Sulla," Adams concluded, "but he is manifestly aping two of Sulla's tricks, holding out proposals of [peace] terms and bribing soldiers to desert.... He is endeavoring to make a Fimbria of somebody."

The history of Sulla's campaigns provided Adams with a unique insight into the military vulnerability of a republic. The Roman republic had been plunged into turmoil, not only by the corruption and reckless ambition of its leaders but more immediately by a so-called "Social War" against former Italian allies who now demanded Roman citizenship. Republics, Adams knew, depended on the patriotism of independent farmers who had come to understand the value of liberty; Howe—like Sulla—undercut republican stability and patriotism by manipulating the loyalties of the rootless and uncommitted loyalist and Hessian mercenary troops. "Many troops from Pennsylvania, Maryland, and Virginia," Adams worried, "are natives of England, Scotland, and Ireland who have adventured over here" as indentured servants or convict labor; "they have no tie to this country,...no principles.... These things give Howe great opportunities to corrupt and seduce them."

The Roman commitment to moderation may have been a reaction against the excesses and fierce hostilities that rent the republic during its last century. Adams's republicanism, expressed in this appeal to Roman history, was a call for courage in the direst of circumstances. Cicero was Adams's idol. As a young man, thrilled by the challenge of the law but torn by self-doubt, Adams read Cicero's admonition to "go forward" and "bend your energies to that study which engages you." More than any other writer Cicero helped Adams integrate and harmonize ambition, desire for fame, humility in the face of an uncertain world, and detachment and calm in the face of crisis. It was natural for Adams to repair to the history of republican Rome for an understanding of evil and for models of responsible statesmanship.

RELIGION

Calvinist Christianity also claimed to possess an authoritative understanding of human weakness and a special insight into the workings of Providence. Therefore, Congregationalist, Presbyterian, and Dutch Reformed patriot clergymen fortified humility with divine boldness to articulate another version of republican moderation. John Witherspoon's sermon preached on May 17, 1776, *The Dominion of Providence over the Passions of Men*, was the most widely read Calvinist justification of the Revolution. Declaring that God's power is absolute, and that God uses the passions of men to serve divine purposes, Witherspoon combined a Calvinist understanding of sinful human nature with a republican appeal for libertarian solidarity. The people should defend their liberty through force of arms because, if their cause was just, it was already assured of divine assistance. And if it was not just, God in some inscrutable way would still use the American struggle against Britain to advance the Kingdom of Christ. The specific contribution that God made to the American cause was the assurance that British rulers "were men and therefore liable to all the selfish bias inseparable from human nature." Thus British coercion was explainable as human selfishness, a condition Britain could no more overcome than Americans could be expected to tolerate. But there was also a divine political logic at work: God was using British tyranny as a means of bringing Americans to repentance.

In Presbyterian terms, the patriots were still blinded by sin but were groping in the direction Providence must be leading them. This was a recognition, as the Presbyterian layman, David Ramsay put it, "that the happiness of the people is the end and object of all government. The wondering world has beheld the smiles of America on the numerous sons of America, resolving to die or be free. Perhaps this noble example, like a wide ranging conflagration, may catch from breast to breast, and extend from nation to nation, till tyranny and oppression are utterly extirpated from the face of the earth."

The role of national moral leadership suited Presbyterians well, perhaps too well. The Presbyterian religious witness became slightly warped during the Revolution, as clergymen like Witherspoon assumed political roles and unintentionally substituted imperatives of national unity for the duty to build a spiritual kingdom. Witherspoon combined Scottish Common Sense moralism, republican communal discipline, and Calvinist theology into a helter-skelter creed of Revolutionary zeal. When the war ended, he fully expected a new generation of leaders—many of them his own Princeton students—to lay the foundations of a new nation in which "piety and virtue" would become "the standard of public honor." Such a society, he predicted, "will enjoy the greatest inward peace, the greatest national happiness, and in every outward struggle will discover the greatest constitutional strength."

The trouble with that prescription was that it burdened theology with political tasks and substituted the new Scottish ethics for traditional political theory in ways that diluted both theology and ethics. Nevertheless, Witherspoon became the authoritative moralist of the Revolution and a prime example of the appeal of moderation.

WASHINGTON

During the long military struggle for independence, George Washington came to embody and symbolize the power of Revolutionary moderation. Perhaps sensing that his physique, horsemanship, demeanor, and reputation for rectitude made him a powerful symbolic presence among the leaders of the Revolution, Washington accentuated a monumental appearance and manner. His self-created iconography—the conformity of portraits, statues, and public impressions to the image he probably sought to convey—made Washington the man into an ideological message.

The core of that message—if it was a deliberate one—and the manifest essence of his leadership, Edmund S. Morgan wrote in *The Genius of George Washington* (1980), was a carefully preserved balance between common humanity and personal reserve. "Be easy and condescending [meaning genuinely modest] in your deportment to your officers," he advised a young Virginian colonel in 1775, "but not too familiar, lest you subject yourself to a want in that respect which is necessary to support a proper command." Eighteen years later, he gave the same advice to his plantation manager at Mount Vernon on supervising overseers: "To treat them civilly is no more than what all men are entitled to, but my advice to you is to keep them at a proper distance, for they will grow upon familiarity in proportion as you will sink in authority." At the Constitutional Convention, the supremely self-confident Gouverneur Morris bet Alexander Hamilton that he could penetrate the general's famous reserve. Bowing before Washington and proclaiming how glad he was to see the general "look so well," Morris then placed his hand on Washington's shoulder while a crowd of other delegates watched in horrified fascination. "The response," Morgan writes, "was immediate and icy. Washington reached up, removed the hand, stepped back, and fixed his eyes in silence on Morris, until Morris retreated abashed into the crowd."

Behind this careful balance between openness and constraint must have been Washington's own vulnerability. Somewhere in his early experience—no biographer has yet shown where—Washington apparently learned that his strongest traits—ambition, boldness, intelligence, and loyalty—could destroy him if he employed them casually. His negative assessment of Charles Lee hinged on this insight. Lee was entirely too willing to improvise a new kind of decentralized warfare without regard for the unpredictable social and psychological consequences. Two of Washington's most important command decisions in the Revolutionary War involved a trade-off between the passion he feared and the reason that he could not ignore.

The first of these was his recommendation to Congress of Nathanael Greene as commander of the southern division of the Continental army. Congress and the states controlled, between them, all military appointments. Washington had built up a fund of good will and trust by always acknowledging this civilian control of his army, even when it saddled him with incompetents. Only once—in the case of Nathanael Greene—did he even try to influence an appointment. Luckily for him, Congress agreed. Greene understood better than Washington the irregular partisan, or guerilla, warfare spreading around the edges of the conventional conflict. And he was more willing to capitalize on the fighting done by irregular bands of fighting men and more imaginative about using local state militia to supplement Continental units. Though Washington shielded his thinking on this point—as he did on all others—he probably knew that opposing Cornwallis in the Carolinas in 1781 would require a theater-of-war commander like Greene, who used strategy and tactics that Washington himself found distasteful.

Then, just as Greene's harrying tactics had driven Cornwallis to distraction and convinced him that the war in the Carolinas was unwinnable until tidewater Virginia was subdued, Washington had a second fundamental decision forced upon him. He and the Comte de Rochambeau, commander of the French troops encamped in Rhode Island, received a message from the French admiral, the Comte de Grasse, that the French fleet—twenty-seven ships that carried 5,500 French soldiers—would enter Chesapeake Bay in force in September 1781. De Grasse directed Washington and Rochambeau to bring their armies there for a decisive encounter. Washington wanted de Grasse to help him capture New York City, and he shuddered at the risks of an overland troop movement from New England and New York to

Virginia. But he knew that he had no alternative. The French would not invest so much of their army and sea power in the American cause again, and the fiscal expedients that Congress and the states had been using to finance the war were nearing exhaustion.

Within a week of receiving de Grasse's plans, Washington and Rochambeau readied 7,000 troops to march south. Washington directed the Marquis de Lafayette, who commanded a small contingent of Continental troops in Virginia, to keep Cornwallis from leaving Yorktown. French ships carrying artillery slipped through the British naval blockade off Rhode Island and brought cannons to Yorktown. To make Clinton think that an assault on New York was imminent, Washington used the route such an attack would have followed in his southward march, thus persuading Clinton to prepare his defenses instead of marching out from New York City to disrupt the American and French line of march. By the time the siege of Yorktown began in early October, Washington had 5,700 Continentals, 3,200 militiamen, and 7,800 French troops, against 8,000 British, Hessian, and loyalist defenders. Cut off from naval relief, his earthworks pounded by French artillery, and outnumbered two to one, Cornwallis quickly surrendered. Washington's desperate need in 1781 coincided with opportunities fraught with peril. His decisions in that dilemma were a model of moderate self-denial and reasoned risk-taking.

Radicalism

The balancing of Revolutionary means and ends, which was the hallmark of moderation, did not function uniformly during the War for Independence. Where elite patriot leadership was weakest, and where British efforts to destabilize patriot regimes enjoyed the greatest success, moderation gave way to a more radical, a more self-consciously republican understanding of the stakes of the conflict. Some historians argue that the War for Independence was everywhere a radicalizing process, that beneath the appearance of moderate leadership lay an exhilarating new sense of democratic competence in large parts of the new nation.

Two regions illustrate particularly well both the radicalizing of the periphery of Revolutionary society, which most historians acknowledge, and also the undermining of traditional conceptions of order throughout the new republic, which Gordon S. Wood detects in *The Radicalism of the American Revolution* (1992). One was the Delmarva peninsula on the eastern shore of Chesapeake Bay, the other, the Carolina backcountry.

The eastern shore counties of Delaware, Maryland, and Virginia chafed under the domination of neighboring patriot elites on the western shore and in Pennsylvania. They resisted taxation, the military draft, and the operation of the court systems of the new regime. Virginia, Delaware, and Maryland lacked the military manpower and the stomach to impose Revolutionary discipline on the peninsula. Moreover, the region had attracted newly arrived Methodist itinerant preachers who knew little about the conflict between Britain and the colonies beyond the fact that their leader, John Wesley, had denounced the Revolution. Preaching to impromptu crowds of slaves, free blacks, and poor whites, the Methodist preachers condemned the war against Britain as a vain and selfish distraction from the serious work of hearing and following God's call to repentance. When a Tory raiding party descended on the home of Constable Robert Appleton, a patriot, they destroyed legal documents pertaining to alleged loyalists and then, with a fine sense of symbolism, punished Appleton by forcing him to read aloud a Methodist sermon and submit to being whipped by a black man. After its formal organization as the American Methodist Church in 1784, the church grew rapidly in size and influence. After 1819 the Methodists modified their opposition to slavery. But throughout the 1790s, the Methodists were a despised sect known for their opposition to slavery and tainted by Toryism.

The Tory commonfolk on the Delmarva peninsula were not counterrevolutionaries seeking to drive the patriots from power. They were dangerous because they called into question the Lockean claim that Britain had violated the compact between the rulers and the ruled and thus denied the Revolution its claim to massive popular support. Grassroots Tory deviance strengthened a republican justification for revolution, which held that a desperate tyrant will usually find a way to deceive some of his subjects and adopt a policy of divide and rule. Further evidence that evangelical folk religion was a current running counter to the Revolution came from the northern counties of Massachusetts—the future state of Maine—and New Hampshire and Vermont. A Baptist revival going on in the maritime region of Canada, led by the charismatic preacher Henry Alline, spilled across the border into New England with a message of liberation from sin. Alline and his converts spoke of being "ravished" by the Holy Spirit and experiencing "divine ecstacy."

The Delmarva Methodists and the northern New England Free Will Baptists exploited the weakening of cultural and religious authority in well-established centers like Boston, Hartford, Annapolis, and Philadelphia. These groups were the vanguard of a democratic, unlettered, exuberant revivalism that would transform American religious life between the Revolution and the age of Jackson—a process described in Nathan O. Hatch, *The Democratization of American Christianity* (1989). The inability of moderate, elite Revolutionary leadership to secure the allegiance of the evangelical commonfolk in some frontier regions helped precipitate a pervasive "crisis of authority in popular culture," which fragmented religious leadership for decades to come.

The British reconquest of Georgia in 1778 and South Carolina two years later inaugurated a desperate struggle for the very life of the Revolution that spread into North Carolina in 1781. Here the war spilled over from the formal battlefields, beyond the control of British and American commanders and into the civilian populace, where irregular soldiers resorted to guerilla warfare. The torture and murder of prisoners, abuse and terrorizing of noncombatants, and the desperate search by both sides for techniques of fighting irregular warfare all sharpened the ideological stakes of the conflict.

Thoughtful figures in both camps understood that the new military realities in the South from 1779 to 1782 had changed the nature of society itself and required a new kind of moral discourse. Samuel Eusebius McCorkle, the Rowan County, North Carolina, Presbyterian minister, called the backcountry struggle an "invasive" conflict in which the horror of war struck deeply into the lives of families, communities, and churches. McCorkle was an ardent republican Revolutionary, but in 1782 he denounced North Carolina patriots for plundering the homes of Tories. Pointing to an Israelite soldier in the book of Joshua who looted silver and gold and vessels of brass and iron, McCorkle drew a republican moral: economic enterprise might invigorate a society, but the process of enrichment had a corrosive underside and had to be disciplined by the public good. In partisan war, he warned, the line between self-interest and criminal greed was perilously thin.

Likewise, a loyalist writer in Georgia, John J. Zubly, also a Presbyterian minister, saw a hideous pattern in Revolutionary violence—"The ghosts of the slain, every drop of innocent blood you [patriots] spilt, every act of violence you concurred in or committed,...every injured widow's groan and every orphan's tear whom you have forced or seduced"—these outrages beseech God, at the final judgment, to punish those who resorted to violent rebellion to gain selfish political advantages. Zubly noted sadly the dynamic of the Revolution itself: its self-justifying use of force, the way coercion expanded outward until it overwhelmed even the weak and helpless, and the patriots' willingness to pay any price, moral or material, to insure the permanence of their new regime.

Thomas Burke, an Irish immigrant who represented North Carolina in the Continental Congress and served as governor in 1781–1782, made the most determined effort to understand what republicanism was doing to the Revolutionary War and what war did to his republican credo. In Congress, Burke had been the most adamant champion of each state's right to pursue its own destiny and make its own decisions. As governor in the chaotic months after Cornwallis marched through North Carolina, he faced a resurgent loyalist force led by David Fanning, which conducted raids, rescued Tory prisoners from jail, and kidnapped patriot officials during the summer and fall of 1781. Burke realized that sending troops against Fanning was futile and that the state had to endure irregular warfare until a shift in the fortunes of war in the Chesapeake Bay area brought the advantage back to the Americans. Before that happened, Burke himself was taken prisoner, eventually escaped, and resumed the post of governor. Nathanael Greene rebuked Burke on the ground that his action jeopardized the safety of American officers who were still held by the British. Burke gave Greene a republican answer. Officers alone did not deserve a privileged status during a people's war; everyone, including part-time militiamen—including civil officials like the governor—possessed equal dignity and had an equal stake in the conflict.

Then Burke gave a particularly republican twist to his argument. Militiamen deserved as much credit as regulars, Burke pointedly told Greene, because both kinds of soldiers were engaged in a pursuit of glory, and such pursuit unavoidably destabilized society. The losers in the race for glory were likely to become desperate men. Thus to protect society from men disillusioned in their own quests for civic distinction, government ought to treat all equally. Writing to another

Irish-born patriot leader, Burke explained why stability depended upon social equality and moral courage:

> In a country where power is in many hands and fluctuating among many hands, the spirit and operation of the government will always depend upon...the manners and moral principles of the people...Are the people needy, rapacious, of low and servile recreation? Narrow, prejudiced, and illiberal? Averse to labor and industry? Familiar with crimes and unaccustomed to restraint? If they be so, no form of government can give security.

Having lived through a destructive and psychologically terrifying war, Burke was uncertain in 1782 whether republicanism could survive in America. His was a pessimism deeply ingrained in the history of republicanism. But like other republicans, he knew of no other acceptable way for power to be held except in "many...fluctuating hands."

Conclusion: Athens and the Precariousness of Republics

Burke's pessimistic lament echoed Pericles' famous funeral oration about civil virtue in fifth-century Athens. While Machiavelli taught civic humanists from the Renaissance to the eighteenth century to look to the Roman republic for a model of a society jeopardized by its inability to live up to its own high moral standards, Madison considered Athens a better source of historical guidance. As Paul A. Rahe explains in *Republics, Ancient and Modern* (1992), Thucydides taught Madison that the Athenian polis was "extraordinarily well governed" under Pericles, a statesman of "rank, intelligence, and evident integrity" who was capable of "restraining the people in the manner of free men." Because Pericles' motives were known to be worthy, he had "no need to say anything solely in order to please the *demos.* When in boldness the people bordered on *hubris*, he could admonish them; when in despair they lost heart, he could restore their spirits. 'He was not led by them,' [Rahe quotes a contemporary of Pericles], 'but they [were led] by him.'"

At the same time, Madison sensed Athens's moral vulnerability. The Delian League, Athens's commercial alliance with smaller city states, rested on bribery and economic domination. Madison equated

Athens's imperial arrogance to that of American slaveholders: "Dependent colonies are to the superior state not [that of] children and parent but...that of slave and master, and have the same effect with slavery upon the character of the superior." Like slaveholders, the citizens of an imperial community such as Athens "cherish pride, luxury, and vanity." Madison concluded that this jostling of interests and passions—even within a framework of self-government and conscientious virtue—had compromised Athenian democracy and might well do so to the American republic. Thomas Burke harbored the same fear.

President George Washington, statue by William Rush. *Courtesy Independence National Park Collection, Philadelphia*.

CHAPTER SIX

Revolutionary Constitutionalism and Disciplining Ideological Energy, 1783–1801

J. G. A. Pocock helped initiate the ideological interpretation of the Revolution, as was noted in Chapter One, by reading a paper at a conference in New Zealand in 1964 about republican ideology in eighteenth-century England. Eleven years later, he set the capstone on this scholarly work by publishing *The Machiavellian Moment: Florentine Political Thought and the Atlantic Republican Tradition* (1975), which discovered the reemergence of classical republicanism as a political creed from the Renaissance to the presidency of Thomas Jefferson. For Pocock, the "Machiavellian moment" is the recurring though rare occasion in which people—who have inherited a political heritage stretching back to late fifteenth-century Florence—choose between building a powerful, economically aggressive society at the cost of corruption and cynicism or, instead, preserving an older and simpler tradition of decentralized social authority purchased with the coin of self-conscious civic virtue and candid public discourse.

The drafting, ratification, and implementation of the United States Constitution, between 1787 and 1794, was, for Pocock, a Machiavellian moment, just as the years from 1679 to 1721—from the Exclusion controversy to rise of Walpole—had been a British Machiavellian moment. As Machiavelli had looked back to Cicero and Cato to understand the death of a republic, and Sidney, Molesworth, and Trenchard had looked back to Renaissance political theory to discern the nexus between power and corruption, so American republicans such as

Jefferson and Madison in the 1780s and 1790s looked back to their ideological forebears among the Commonwealthmen and the country ideology for an understanding of the vulnerability and hidden genius of their new republic.

To understand how revolutionary Pocock's formulation was, and is, readers must attend to his belief that in the Machiavellian moment "virtue can develop only in time, but is always threatened by corruption by time." By this he means that the Machiavellian moment is a *kairotic* moment—a moment of timeless significance rather than simply a straightforward happening in chronological time. Pocock's former student, John M. Murrin, applied the Machiavellian moment hypothesis directly to the Constitution in a paper written in 1976 and published in Pocock ed., *Three British Revolutions, 1641, 1688, 1776* (1980). There Murrin suggested that in both Walpolean England and in Madisonian America the crises that made ideological time stand still were economic as well as political. And because economic choices made in times of transition profoundly affect people's lives for better or ill, they were moral crises as well.

Was there a Machiavellian moment at the core of the American constitutional founding? Not surprisingly, historians disagree, but these disagreements may well contain the seeds of a new consensus.

The "Machiavellian Moment" Debate

For Drew R. McCoy, in *The Elusive Republic: Political Economy in Jeffersonian America* (1980), the Machiavellian moment was the "specific configuration of assumptions, fears, beliefs, and values that shaped a vision of expansion across...the American continent," envisioning a social transformation that could save the nation from "political corruption and social decay." The economic history of republics convinced many American Revolutionary leaders that agricultural stability—the preservation of a society of yeoman farmers—and a limited amount of commercial stimulus could prevent the republic from succumbing to disintegration or despotism which, ever since the Greek city states, had been the fate of republics. But during the early 1790s Hamilton's program for using the national debt, customs and excise duties, and the Bank of the United States to expand and reward investment particularly alarmed Virginians and heightened their fear that economic nationalism would subvert republican virtue. Jefferson and Madison noted Hamilton's preference for British institutions and forms of social order, his admiration for centralized, expert statecraft, and they correctly suspected him of tilting United States foreign policy toward British interests as a necessary inducement to the maintenance of a high level of trade imports from Britain, the customs duties of which were income needed to underwrite the national debt. In short, Hamilton sought to establish what appeared to his critics to be a client-state relationship with Great Britain as a necessary precondition for the maturation of American society. The "spectre of Walpole," which Madison and Jefferson detected in Hamilton's program, thus bound Madison and Jefferson together and informed the ideology of a diverse band of political supporters in the Republican party from its formation in 1793 until the presidency of James Monroe, 1817–1825.

Challenging the concept of the Machiavellian moment are a group of scholars, including Thomas Pangle, Isaac Kramnick, Joyce Appleby, and Jack P. Greene. Pangle, in *The Spirit of Modern Republicanism: The Moral Vision of the American Founders and the Philosophy of Locke* (1988), argues that Locke was himself a republican who absorbed fully the Renaissance, civic humanist celebration of social virtue. But for Pangle, Locke's politics did not call for heroic service to the community so much as it advocated "a capacity for protest, resistance, and even risk" rooted in a "sober sense of dignity and self-respect," virtues which were individual, Protestant, and closely related to life, liberty, and property. In a study of the modes of political discourse at the time of the Constitution, Kramnick discerns a republican language of virtue and imperilled liberty and also three other vibrant forms of political expression—Lockean individualism, Protestant civic discipline, and the new language of statecraft.

Joyce Appleby also doubts that there was a Machiavellian moment because she does not define the economic prospects of the United States in the 1790s in terms of either agrarian stability *or* commercially driven expansion. She views the two as integrally related. "The material base upon which Jefferson built his vision of America," she writes, was the tremendous expansion in grain production in the middle Atlantic states during the post-Revolutionary generation. Here agriculture drove commercial expansion by creating an export crop, stimulating urban economies in Baltimore, Philadelphia, and New York, and rewarding farmers who were willing to take financial risks in the interest of greater productivity.

"Agriculture did not figure in [Jefferson's] plans as a venerable form of production giving shelter to a traditional way of life," Appleby contends, "rather he was responsive to every possible change in cultivation, processing, and marketing that would enhance its profitability." Working with opportunities readily at hand just as Hamilton had done with debt and speculation—the settlement of the trans-Appalachian West, the removal of hostile Indians and subversive European agents, and the new ethos of enterprise and innovation among farmers and merchants—Jefferson found what Appleby calls "a new conception of human nature that affirmed the reciprocal influences of freedom and prosperity." The framers of the Constitution, she believes, saw this connection clearly, and they sought to make the Constitution into a fundamental law that severely restricted the range of governmental power over individuals and groups.

Appleby's vision of economic dynamism in a republican society, fostered by individual choice and competition, truly made the Constitution an economic document, but not in the same sense that Charles A. Beard had suggested in 1913 when he accused the framers of protecting the value of their investments in Continental Congress securities. Rather it was an economic document because, as Jack P. Greene writes, it recognized the supremacy of "the private realm" in American life: "The American people [advocates of the Constitution contended] had to be freed from the intrusive and obstructive interventions of the majorities of state legislatures before commerce could achieve its full potential as a bountiful arena for the free exertion of individual talents and resources." Rather than relegating commerce to the restricted role of supporting small producer agriculture, which McCoy found in Jeffersonian thought, Appleby and Greene conceive of commerce conducted by "undifferentiated individuals" as an expression of individualism in the new republic.

Generally sympathetic to the critics of the Machiavellian moment thesis but also concerned with the economic content of the constitutional crisis are Forrest McDonald, Cathy D. Matson, and Peter N. Onuf. McDonald, in *Novus Ordo Seclorum: The Intellectual Origins of the Constitution* (1985) and Matson and Onuf, in *A Union of Interests: Political and Economic Thought in Revolutionary America* (1990), examine the commercial and economic intentions of the framers. Mc-

Donald discusses their use of the new science of political economy, and he treats political economy in anti-Pocockian terms as a value-free discipline that provided American leaders with a whole new menu of choices and analytical tools. In this examination of the ideas of Thomas Malthus, Adam Smith, Sir James Steuart, and Bernard Mandeville, McDonald demonstrates that their ideas about money, trade, investment, and economic regulation composed a new kind of ideological discussion that, no less than republicanism or Lockean liberalism, voiced a vision of the future.

Turning from ideas to behavior, Matson and Onuf argue that the threat of economic disintegration within a weak confederacy made a durable union of the states imperative. Americans needed a government complex enough to foster "industrious activity directed toward future rewards." Together, the language of political economy (with its emphasis on strategies of social change) and the goal of releasing economic energies on a continental, rather than a state, scale predisposed the framers to define the nation's needs in a common language and to experiment with various means for reaching an agreed-upon goal.

Matson and Onuf present new evidence that economic interest groups, which were frustrated in the mid-1780s by irresponsible state legislatures and trade stagnation, considered breaking the country into three regional republics—each with shared economic interests. Regional disunion of the Confederation, Matson and Onuf caution, was not disruptive or reactionary; rather, breaking the republic into regional sovereign units was an intelligent stop-gap attempt to curtail the power of state legislatures while at the same time fostering economic enterprise.

The problem of restoring economic health and political responsibility, as McDonald shows, prompted the most intellectually urbane American leaders—Madison, Adams, and Hamilton among them—to apply concepts of political economy to the work of constitutionalism. From Bernard Mandeville, *The Fable of the Bees: Private Vices, Publick Benefits* (1714) they learned how economic activity cancels out human vices and leaves a residue of socially redemptive activity. Sir James Steuart, *Principles of Political Oeconomy* (1767) examined for the first time the interaction of land, agriculture, money, labor, and commerce and noted the crucial role of a monetized debt in building a powerful state (that is, a national debt with revenue sources earmarked for payment of the interest on the debt). Smith, as is noted in Chapter Three, emphasized the role of market mechanisms to regulate the economy and, to a lesser extent, on moral sentiments to constrain the power of producers. Finally, Thomas Malthus, *Essay...on Population* (1798), which prophesied a famine resulting from overpopulation, confirmed John Adams's dour view that economic scarcity would take its toll on America's slender reserves of civic virtue. Political economists, especially Steuart, deeply influenced Hamilton's thinking about debt and taxation, while Madison drew eclectically on these writers in order to formulate a rather breezy plan for maximizing American economic assets and capitalizing on apparent weaknesses in the British economy.

Political economy was ideological in the sense that it focused the thinking of these American leaders about the nature of power and the legitimate functions of government. Political economy was an aspect of statecraft, one of Kramnick's four categories of public discourse (see above p. 105) which rationalist public officials had begun to articulate in Europe during the seventeenth and eighteenth centuries. The language of statecraft was indeed ideological, but instead of being used to diagnose social pathologies like corruption and tyranny, it now provided the vocabulary to propose strategies for achieving change, and helped to prioritize republican goals.

Pushed away from the center of public discussion by the need to consider hard economic dilemmas, republican ideology now became instrumental. Admittedly, classifying political economy as instrumental—ideology used for a particular social purpose—may well amount to saying that ideology had ceased to be ideological and that political figures had ceased viewing the world through moral perceptions. In his recent article, "Republicanism: The Career of an Idea," *Journal of American History* (1992), Daniel T. Rodgers argues that historians have burdened the concept of ideology with altogether too much psychic and cultural significance, and that by making it explain all of eighteenth-century politics, it ends up explaining nothing. The implication of Rodgers's criticism for the late 1780s and 1790s is that republican ideology had ceased to charge the imaginations of American political leaders as it had in the 1770s. Gordon S. Wood, in a celebrated passage from *Creation of the American Republic*, pinpointed this "end of ideology" by observing that classical Whig ideas of the 1770s

> sought to understand politics, as it had all of life, by capturing in an integrated, ordered, changeless ideal the totality and complexity of life.... In

> such an ideal there could be only potential energy, no kinetic energy....By destroying this ideal, Americans placed a new emphasis on the piecemeal and the concrete in politics at the expense of order and completeness.

Bernard Bailyn does not perceive quite so sharp a demarcation between Revolutionary ideology and post-Revolutionary realism. The framers and defenders of the Constitution, he told the American Historical Association in 1987, had to accomplish four interrelated tasks: first, to "convince" their critics that the Articles of Confederation had created a dangerous power vacuum; second, to demonstrate that the new federal system and the extensive powers of Congress were the correct remedy; third, to insure the people that the new nation would not simply absorb the states into a centralized unitary state; and, fourth,

> they had to reach back into the sources of the received tradition [*i.e.*, republicanism], confront ancient fears that had lain at the heart of the ideological origins of the Revolution, and identify and reexamine the ancient formulations that stood in the way of present necessities: take these ideas apart and where necessary rephrase them, reinterpret them—not to reject them in favor of a new paradigm, a new structure of thought, but reapply them and bring them up to date.

The conflict between "ancient fears" and "present necessities" was central to the drafting and ratification of the Federal Constitution. This chapter will examine the rethinking of those fears and necessities, the cleaving to and the pulling away from an ideological understanding of the American Revolution.

Republican Tensions

In these two categories of political thought—the libertarian tradition of the antifederalists and the constitutionalism of the federalists—Bailyn located the great social divide of the 1780s and 1790s. It was a fissure that had been implicit in republicanism itself. As Richard R. Beeman has recently argued, republicanism "conveyed a double message": on one hand, it held that power was dangerous because it could be directed against the people by a handful of oppressors, but on the other hand, virtue, the only antidote to oppressive power, "was likely to be found among the natural aristocracy." Therefore, the wise few had to govern the foolish many—albeit with their consent. The essence of republicanism was this tension between the mobilization of the many—through military service, voting, land distribution, religious appeals for sacrifice—and the use of constitutional means to sift out the virtuous few for political responsibility. In examining the cleavage between ideological purity and constitutional practice in post-Revolutionary America, it is important to remember the reciprocity and interdependence of these two impulses. Purists needed innovations to criticize; reformers needed abuses to remedy. Ideology thus fortified two different social worlds, one in which virtue was scarce (the glass half empty) and another in which the supply of virtue was at least adequate to the needs of the people (the glass half full). Nowhere were these two worlds so intimately joined as in western Massachusetts during Shays's Rebellion (1786–1787), and nowhere were the ideological stakes higher than in the Virginia controversy over religious liberty (1776–1786).

SHAYS'S REBELLION

In western Massachusetts, the economic legacy of the Revolution was a hard one. The closing of the British West Indies to American shipping in 1784 hurt Massachusetts shippers badly. The arrival of British mercantile agents with cheap goods and long lines of credit squeezed Boston merchants. The Massachusetts legislature moved quickly to begin payments on its public debt in hopes of converting the debt from a liability into an asset, but there was not enough coin in circulation to meet the demand of bond holders who needed payment in specie. When Congress, in September 1785, requisitioned the states for an immediate payment toward reduction of the nation's indebtedness to French and Dutch creditors, Massachusetts—with its large population and burgeoning commerce—bore a disproportionately large share of this (national) burden.

Knowing that failure to meet the requisition might push the Confederation into insolvency, the Massachusetts legislature feared for the viability of the state's commercial economy if it did not comply. As a result, the legislature refused all entreaties that it reduce taxes or issue more paper money. The chief impact of this policy was to force everyone in the credit chain to demand repayment from their debtors so they in turn could satisfy their creditors. If this meant sending hard-pressed farmers to jail or foreclosure on farms pledged as collateral, the holders of this debt often felt they had no choice.

Daniel Shays was a Revolutionary War veteran who denounced the state for disregarding the needs of thousands of farmers for tax relief, more plentiful specie, and temporary protection from foreclosure. One of Shays's supporters, Adam Wheeler of Hubbardstown, defended the mob takeover of the Worcester County courts by explaining that he "had no intentions to destroy the publick government" but only "to have the...courts...suspended, to prevent such abuses as have of late taken place,...valuable and industrious members of society dragged from their families to prison, to the great damage not only of their families but the community at large."

The most important ideological current in Shays's Rebellion was the conflict between creditors, who knew that the entire society had a supreme stake in a properly funded, well-managed public debt, on one hand, and people like Adam Wheeler, who, in true republican fashion, saw the good of the community being sacrificed to the interests of individuals exercising their natural right to pursue and possess property.

Recent scholarship—Robert A. Gross, ed., *In Debt to Shays: The Bicentennial of an Agrarian Rebellion* (1993)—reveals the moral complexity and irony of the rebellion. Both sides believed their fiscal prescriptions would serve the public good. The Shaysites saw the cup of virtue half empty. Defenders of law and order saw it half full. In towns where Shays's supporters were dominant, the pulpits of Congregationalist churches were more often than not vacant, and dissenter sects were weak. Thus economic stress seems to have coincided with anxiety about the sacred order of the organic New England community and mirrored anxieties deep within society.

The Shaysites were Regulators like those in the Carolinas before the Revolution who took power temporarily into their own hands for the good of society rather than usurping authority for any personal gain. Jackson Turner Main, in *Political Parties before the Constitution* (1973), has labeled the contending sides in Confederation era politics "cosmopolitans" and "localists," and he defines cosmopolitans as individuals with educational, business, and familial ties outside their own state and town.

The line between the wider and the local worlds was subtler and less distinct than Main found it. The worlds of creditor and debtor, for example, merged in the civil courts. Here judges often sensed the futility of driving defendants to the wall and sought ways to help them postpone debt payment until their cash flow increased. Debtors who hid assets from the court to avoid payment to their creditors could be jailed, but once the court determined genuine insolvency, the law afforded debtors protection from imprisonment. Nor were the civil courts biased on behalf of all creditors. Judges expected wealthy creditors to show patience, and it was the smaller merchants who could not afford to show leniency who pressed legal remedies most ruthlessly. Judges knew that jailing a civil defendant cut him off from the livelihood needed to meet debt obligations to other creditors, so that the good of the community required patience from the court as well as flexibility from multiple creditors. Only when faced with imminent financial ruin themselves was it in the interest of many creditors to use the courts as collection agencies. "Under the control of no single class," Robert Gross writes, "the courts may well have served the interests of none."

Men of property throughout America responded to Shays's Rebellion with horror and disgust. These reactions accelerated the movement for a constitution strong enough to maintain public tranquility. But the deeper connection between Shays's Rebellion and the Constitution had to do with public debt rather than disorder. What the trade depression and debt crisis of the mid-1780s demonstrated was that no single state—not even one with as dynamic an economy and as committed to helping reduce the national debt as Massachusetts—could materially improve the public credit of the nation. Only a new government with the sole responsibility for the public credit of the United States could in the long run deal with the problems of debt, taxes, money supply, and judicial authority that had precipitated Shays's Rebellion in the first place.

CHURCH AND STATE IN VIRGINIA

Virginia was the scene of another republican struggle over the location and preservation of virtue in post-Revolutionary America. In 1776, the Virginia Declaration of Rights had held

> [1] that religion, or the duty we owe our *CREATOR*, and the manner of discharging it, can be directed only by reason and conviction, not by

> force or violence; [2] and therefore, all men are equally entitled to the free exercise of religion, according to the dictates of conscience; and [3] that it is the mutual duty of all to practice Christian forbearance, love, and charity toward each other.

The "discharge of religious duties" clause articulated the approved republican way of claiming a natural right; the "free exercise of religion clause" extended the natural right of religious liberty to all moved by the dictates of conscience; and the "mutual duty" clause implied Lockean reciprocity among contending religious persuasions. For more than a decade thereafter, the General Assembly struggled to draft legislation that institutionalized Christian piety, republicanism, and civility in the Old Dominion.

In 1779, the legislature considered what Thomas E. Buckley calls "the legislation of virtue." In proper republican fashion, the authors of "A Bill Concerning Religion" proposed a four-fold legal process for the recovery of depleted social virtue: a doctrinal test for churches incorporated under the law, guarantees of clerical orthodoxy, prohibitions against unruly conduct in worship, and financial assessment of taxpayers to support ministerial salaries. The doctrinal test—a five-part definition of a Christian, which was taken from the South Carolina statute of 1778—emphasized belief in a "future state of rewards and punishments" but said nothing about grace or salvation. The guarantee of clerical orthodoxy was a long list of priestly duties and pious attitudes, and the requirement of political good conduct proscribed "disrespectful" or "seditious" language in church services. Finally, the bill provided for each property-owning church member to pay a public assessment toward the salary of his clergyman, and all not designating church affiliation to contribute a like sum to a common fund for distribution to all churches.

The War for Independence prevented action on the 1779 bill, but in 1784 advocates of assessment had drafted a tighter statute, "[A Bill] Establishing a Provision for Teachers of the Christian Religion." With the powerful backing of Patrick Henry, this bill seemed certain to pass, until Baptist and Presbyterian churches mobilized against it. Hundreds of petitions, bearing several thousand signatures, flooded the legislature. Sensing the change in the public temper, Madison composed and distributed his "Memorial and Remonstrance against Religious Assessments." As an alternative to the assessment bill, Madison resurrected one of five bills on religion that had been proposed in 1779 as bills 82–86 of a general revision of the Virginia legal code. This bill, which Madison wanted to substitute for the assessment measure was bill 82, Jefferson's "Statute for Religious Liberty," which in sweeping rationalist language proscribed any action by government compelling anyone "to frequent or support any religious worship, place, or ministry" through taxation or civil incapacitation: "To compel a man to furnish contributions of money for the propagations of opinions which he disbelieves *and abhors* is sinful and tyrannical."

Patrick Henry's elevation to the governorship in 1784 removed the assessment bill's strongest champion from the debate at a crucial moment and enabled Madison to secure passage of Jefferson's Statute, precluding assessment altogether. Years later, Jefferson called his Statute and the First Amendment "a wall of separation" between church and state. But it should be noted that bills 83–86, which both Jefferson and Madison endorsed as a package along with bill 82, sanctioned not separation of church and state, but rather a moderate regulation of religious practice by the state. Bill 83 protected Episcopal vestry property; bill 84 outlawed unnecessary labor on the Sabbath; bill 85 sanctioned public days of prayer and fasting; and bill 86 allowed civil marriages. The effect of bills 83–86 was to leave the Virginia government room to regulate religion and to sanction certain forms of religious practice as public policy. Modern advocates of church-state separation quote bill 82 out of its legislative context, while modern defenders of school prayer and other civil observances of religion ignore the fact that the Virginia Statute and the First Amendment were intended by their authors to proscribe all nondiscriminatory government aid to churches—the very principle which would have prevailed if Jefferson's bill had not scuttled assessment in 1785.

The choice between assessment and complete religious liberty was a choice between pessimistic republicanism and enlightenment rationalism. The advocates of assessment were transfixed with the specter of earlier republics (Athens and Rome) corrupted by prosperity and thus indifferent to religion and duty. Rationalist champions of religious liberty felt confident that a benevolent creator was indifferent to the manner in which people worshipped and that religious conviction was entirely a matter of private judgment. The evangelicals who supported Madison looked forward to a day when all would believe in the crucified Christ and saw the state as a hindrance to the coming of the kingdom of God. As with creditors and debtors in western Massachusetts, republicanism taught the conservation of virtue, while Locke and the enlightenment maximized the human capacity to act virtuously.

The Great Compromise

Another critical transition in the early republic, and also one in which ideology facilitated a far-reaching change in the structure of government, was the "Great Compromise" of July 16, 1787, in the Constitutional Convention. Until June 20, the delegates had struggled to devise a new Constitution along the lines of the "Virginia Plan," Madison's idea of a national government dominated by the lower house of a powerful legislature: seats in the lower house apportioned according to population, the upper house elected by the lower house, and the legislature empowered to veto state laws. The delegations from the large states were unable to assure colleagues from the small states that they were not about "to be thrown under the domination of the large states." On July 2, 1787, and over Madison's objections, the delegates charged a new committee of eleven members with the task of devising a new basis for continued deliberations. After wrangling over its recommendations, the delegates voted on July 12 to count slaves as three-fifths of free white persons for purposes of apportionment, and on July 16 they voted for apportionment of the lower house according to population, equal representation of the Senate, money bills to initiate in the lower house, and a mandatory census and reapportionment every ten years.

Together, these four provisions constituted "the Great Compromise," and there are at least three distinct interpretations of its meaning. The oldest originated with one of its architects, William Samuel Johnson of Connecticut, and received its modern formulation in Clinton Rossiter, *1787: The Grand Convention* (1966). On June 29, Johnson had warned that deadlock in the convention would be "endless" unless both sides recognized the peculiar symmetry of their positions. Nationalists rightly regarded the states as "districts of people" bound together into a single nation by the struggle for independence from Great Britain; at the same time, the states were each separate "political societies" each with its own security and economic interests, or, in

Rossiter's words, "discrete, self-conscious, indestructable units of political and social organization." "In some respects," Johnson told the Convention, "the states are to be considered in their political capacity and in others as districts of individual citizens.... The two ideas,... instead of being opposed, ought to be combined" by apportioning the House and guaranteeing equal representation in the Senate. Once the delegates accepted Johnson's logic a whole new kind of Constitution became possible. The new formula made *paradox* rather than *consensus* the inner framework of the document; instead of being an operator's manual on government with detailed solutions to foreseeable difficulties, the new Constitution would be, for the most part, a lucid, concise, general essay about the nature and disposition of power.

Lance Banning offers a subtler and less dramatic interpretation of the Great Compromise, one in which Madison himself played an indirect role. Banning agrees with Rossiter that the compromise was a setback for Madison, but he contends that after July 16, Madison accommodated himself to the new approach. Madison did so because his ardor for a strong national government anticipated the federalism of the Great Compromise. Madison, Banning contends, had never been a nationalist bent on centralizing authority in one government. Even his proposal that Congress have the power to veto state laws was intended less to strengthen national authority than it was to save the state legislatures from their own folly.

Madison came to the Constitutional Convention better prepared than any other delegate. During the preceding months he had conducted an exhaustive review of the history of earlier republics and the failings of the American republic under the Articles of Confederation. So long as the states could withhold support from the general government with impunity, and so long as Congress lacked the independent authority to carry out the duties assigned it by the Articles, citizens could have no respect for their own government, no confidence in their capacity for self-government. But Madison had not yet envisioned a federal solution to this problem. When George Mason defined a federal government as one with the power to act directly on the people rather than through the agency of the states, Madison began to grasp the solution to the impotence of the general government: the enumeration of powers of Congress to enact laws binding on each citizen. This discovery did not, Banning insists, make Madison a nationalist; it prompted him to question each proposed federal power as to its necessity to the task of securing the nation's prosperity and security. The Great Compromise had dashed Madison's hope that the Senate would be apportioned by population, so as to make it reflect the will of the people, but when the Convention committed itself to equal representation of the states in the upper house, he did not seek to reduce in any way the concurrent power of the Senate, along with the House, to levy taxes or regulate trade. By the time of the Virginia ratifying convention, Madison took the position that the central government "derives its authority from the [state] governments *and from the same source from which their authority is derived*"—that is, from the people themselves (italics added). Thus popular sovereignty enabled the states to erect over them a federal authority that was not national but nonetheless possessed authority independently of the states. The Great Compromise did not jeopardize the empowering of the federal government, but it did delay Madison's full appreciation of the crucial distinction between national and federal authority.

Where Banning saw Madison teaching others the compatibility of federalism with republicanism, Jack N. Rakove depicts Madison at the Convention learning—teaching himself first and foremost—to comprehend the relationship between representation and republican government. He came to Philadelphia, Rakove declares, convinced of the paramount need to correct the "imbecility" of the Union and the immaturity of the states. "The time had come not only to rescue Congress from the states, but to save the states from themselves."

Rescuing Congress from the states required, in Madison's judgment, proportionate representation of both houses of the new Congress so as to render Congress the voice of the people and not the tool of the states. State governments contributed nothing to the councils of the nation beyond the ambitions and agendas of politicians on the state level. There was nothing inherently wrong with those ambitions and agendas, but in order to legislate, Congress needed to hear from the widest range of interests: "creditors or debtors—rich or poor—husbandmen, merchants, or manufacturers—members of different religious sects—followers of different political leaders—inhabitants of different districts—owners of different kinds of property &c &c." Those were not interests to be placated or selfish factions to be shunned. Republican statecraft meant reconciling the larger, more constructive, more public-spirited of those interests with the national interest. That work should be done by the best-educated and most widely experienced members of society, who could be expected to win seats in the new House of Representatives as well as the Senate. Madison expected the small states to go along with proportionate representation in the Senate because all states, large and small, contained a spectrum of interests. He also expected the small states to look for neighboring allies with similar economies and social systems. All this, Rakove argues, came to Madison as he grappled with the problems of majority rule and the interests of the states.

Making Congress accountable to, and ultimately connected to, the people, Madison warned, would avail little if state governments continued to be captive to the political passions of the moment. For that reason, he continued to advocate a congressional veto on state laws, now suggesting that it be a special power of the Senate. The result of this tough talk about curbing the power of the states was to rekindle the very republican jealousy that Madison wanted to moderate. "It seems as if Pennsylvania and Virginia, by the conduct of their deputies," a delegate from Delaware pointedly said in reference to Madison and his ally James Wilson, "wish to provide a system in which they have an enormous and monstrous influence." Madison must have muttered that what was monstrous was the reckless conduct of the states and the inability of a Congress dependent on the states to act in the national interest. All he could say was that Pennsylvania and Virginia could not have evil designs on other states because states were contrived entities rather than natural political communities.

This cavalier attitude toward the states arose, Rakove argues, because "Madison went to the Convention in the grip of a great intellectual passion: the belief that both the state and national governments must draw their authority from the people and act directly on the people if republican government was to be saved from parochialism and liberty was to flourish. What force softened Madison's suspicions concerning the states? Certainly not the New Jersey Plan, which William Paterson proposed on June 15, 1787, as an alternative to the Virginia Plan. Most delegates recognized immediately that the New Jersey Plan augmented the powers of Congress and added a petulant proposal for Congress to force recalcitrant states to meet their financial obligations to the Union—a wildly impractical scheme that would have discredited the very national authority to which it gave lip service.

The force that eased Madison out of the thrall of his "great intellectual passion" was a suggestion from the aging John Dickinson, who agreed with Madison's diagnosis of the defects of the Union and the responsibility of the Convention to the whole body of the people. But Dickinson distrusted Madison's strategy of settling on representation as the essential remedy to the ills of the confederation. Why not, he asked early in the Convention, start with details like the powers of Congress and consider later the more vexing problem of the quantum of power that Congress needed to represent the people? With Madison opposed, Dickinson's procedural suggestion died. But two weeks later, as the frustration of the small states approached the boiling point, Dickinson took Madison aside and angrily told him, "You now see the consequence of pushing things too far. Some of the members from the small states...are friends to a good national government; but we would sooner submit to a foreign power than...be deprived of an equality of suffrage in both houses of the legislature." Others saw the same bottom line: the New Jersey Plan was not an alternative to the Virginia Plan but a warning that the new Constitution would have to be federal and national at the same time.

Madison made one more dramatic attempt to instruct the delegates on the virtues of representation as the foundation of constitutional reform. On June 30 he offered a compelling but disturbing reason why the large states would not dominate the small ones: "the states [are] divided...not by their size but by other circumstances,...principally their having or not having slaves." Predicting a North-South rather than a large state–small state division, Madison then offered a compromise: apportion the lower house according to the free population and the upper house according to the whole population, free and slave. The next day he went further and predicted that proportional representation in both houses would establish an "equilibrium" between slave and free sections of the country. Far from mollifying his critics, Madison's comments on slavery injected fresh apprehensions into the Convention and speeded the search for a compromise guaranteeing equal representation in the Senate.

In Rakove's view, Madison's "Intellectual passion," his fixation on representation as the key to constitutional reform, was not a dead end; instead, it made the Great Compromise possible by goading other moderate nationalist delegates into devising a comparably elaborate approach. Once they discovered the concept of intrinsic paradox, the framers possessed an insight into constitutionalism with a wide applicability. They could now tackle the vexing problem of ultimate authority—what Madison called "the great desideratum" or requirement of republican government, "some disinterested and dispassionate umpire in disputes between different passions and interests in the state." The solution the framers devised was subtle and indirect. By assigning Congress seventeen specific powers and by denying the states a few dangerous powers, the Constitution kept the two spheres of government from colliding. National laws and treaties were to be "the supreme law of the land," a limp remnant of Madison's proposed veto of state laws. The authors of the Tenth Amendment in 1791 recognized the tilt toward national authority in these provisions and reversed the implied advantage by assigning all powers not granted to Congress nor denied the states "to the states,...or to the people." It would take the Civil War and the Fourteenth Amendment to establish that, in areas of citizenship and equality, the states *were* subordinate.

Banning stresses Madison's classical republicanism in his use of balance and moderation to preserve liberty, while Rakove credits Madison with using the same republican principles to make power the servant rather than the enemy of republican government. Whether the preservation of liberty or the creative use of power was the nobler goal of constitutional government will always depend on how people interpret the Constitution.

Ratification Debate

For the deepest insight into republican constitutionalism, we must turn to the ratification debate and, in particular, the essays that John Jay, James Madison, and Alexander Hamilton wrote in support of its ratification, *The Federalist*. In his contribution to *The Federalist*, Madison sought to refute two antifederalist arguments: first, that the Constitution would foster the growth of factions, and second, that it would place more power in the hands of federal officeholders than human beings could responsibly handle.

To deflect antifederalist fears of greedy, conspiratorial factionalism oozing from every pore of the national government, Madison turned to the "faculty psychology" of the Scottish moral philosopher Thomas Reid, who distinguished between "animal" faculties (appetites, desires, passions) and "rational" faculties (conscience and self-interest). "As long as there remains a connection between [man's] reason and his self-love," Madison explained, "his opinions and his passions will have a reciprocal influence on each other," with passion damaging reason. The Constitution, he argued, was designed to use this tension in order to protect the body politic from the irrationality that men unavoidably bring into political life. For example, stipulating that congressional districts contain upward of thirty thousand inhabitants was meant to insure that representatives be well-known figures with national, rather than purely local, leadership experience. This strategy would, in turn, lessen the influence of "factious tempers," "local prejudices," and "sinister designs."

Reid's faculty psychology also taught Madison that passionate vices like factional greed and political deviousness could be humanized; factions could be asked to temper their own greed by considering the public good and by rewarding those who did so with public esteem and economic benefits. Factions could also be managed in the public interest by close attention to their histories. Not all factions were alike. The smaller a faction, Madison concluded from an extensive study of the history of republics, the more it operated in secrecy and darkness and the more likely it was to be driven by greed and a lust for domination. Conversely, the larger a faction, the more openly it functioned, and the more it served as a coalition of like-minded groups, the more compatible its goals would be with some larger public interest. The powers of Congress gave the national government the means to reward the latter kind of faction and to civilize factions by teasing benevolent tendencies from human enterprise.

"If Publius [the pen name of the authors of *The Federalist*] was rather old fashioned in his distrust of passion," Daniel W. Howe writes in a recent study, "he was quite up to date in his techniques for controlling it." That technique was the Enlightenment idea of balancing hostile actions against each other "like the antagonistic muscles of the body," in Francis Hutcheson's simile. How could an unscrupulous administrator be prevented from usurping power from his colleagues? "The great security," Madison answered, "consists in giving to those who administer each department the necessary constitutional means and personal motives to resist the encroachments of others.... By so contriving the interior structure of the government,...its several constituent parts may, by their mutual relations, be the means of keeping each other in their proper places." This strategy of reliance on "the private interest of every individual" to serve as a "check" on the whole came from John Witherspoon's lectures on moral philosophy at Princeton, which taught that "counterpoise" in political conflict preserved the virtue of a society.

The implementation of the Constitution during the presidencies of Washington and Adams from 1789 to 1801 enabled American political leaders to move still further away from a preoccupation with ideology and to immerse themselves in the practical tasks of setting the nation's finances on a firm footing and conducting foreign policy in a dangerous world. A new era of high-minded statesmanship seemed at hand. The more self-consciously men like Hamilton, Madison, Jefferson, and Washington exercised power—by acting on carefully considered principles—the more they invoked the moral purposes of government and sought to preserve the republican experiment itself. They thus remained embedded in the ideological heritage of the Revolution.

Conclusion: Hamilton, Jefferson, and the Nature of Republicanism

When the first House of Representatives, under Madison's leadership, asked Treasury Secretary Alexander Hamilton to report on the nation's finances, Hamilton seized the opportunity to present a comprehensive plan that included funding the national debt, assuming the states' debts, chartering a private Bank of the United States to manage the debt, issue currency, serve as a depository of governmental funds, and imposing excise taxes and import duties. The unstated provision was the restoration of amicable relations with Great Britain, the only trading partner that could sell enough to America to generate the import-duty revenue needed to fund the debt.

Hamilton's wise and far-sighted proposals and his powerful advocacy secured their legislative enactment, but gradually his behind-the-scenes influence over foreign policy generated suspicion and hostility. Even thoughtful critics like Madison—only recently Hamilton's ally in the ratification struggle—realized that Hamilton had a complex vision of a commercial and industrial nation that needed the combined efforts of private investors and public officials to expand and prosper. An agrarian society of the kind Jefferson apparently yearned to create simply would not generate enough wealth to finance military power and motivate businessmen to engage in risky enterprises.

Behind this strategy for national development—and provoking Madison's and Jefferson's apprehension—was Hamilton's political philosophy, which linked a pessimistic view of human nature to a preference for energetic government: "Take mankind in general, they are vicious," Hamilton told the Constitutional Convention. But as "their passions are ambition and interest;...it will ever be the duty of a wise government to avail itself of those passions, in order to make them subservient to the public good—for these [passions] ever induce us to action." The action that Hamilton felt passionately called to undertake was to establish, in a highly visible way, the authority of the national government to tax its citizens. When farmers in western Pennsylvania—and indeed throughout the West—evaded and then resisted payment of the new excise tax on whiskey, Hamilton seized the opportunity to vindicate the authority of the national government by using armed force. He persuaded a receptive President Washington that it was "absolutely necessary" to send troops to western Pennsylvania to enforce the collection of the whiskey excise.

Hamilton was no autocrat. He was a thoughtful republican theorist as well as a finance minister. He knew that both the power of the ruler and the democratic sentiments of the people were capable of being abused. The problem was that democratic excesses looked benign, while the power of government appeared sinister, even when it was simply doing its job: "A dangerous ambition more often lurks behind the specious mask of a zeal for the rights of the people than under the forbidding appearance of zeal for the firmness and efficiency of government." He did not say that firm, efficient government carried no risk of abuse, but Hamilton did extract from classical republican sources a constraint on executive power: "the love of glory." Stoic writers like Marcus Aurelius and Roman republican heroes like Cato had taught posterity that selfless devotion to the public good earned public leaders a special kind of acclaim that was infinitely more gratifying and desirable than wealth or dominion over others. Washington, who shared this concept of republican duty, recognized it when he said of Hamilton: "By some he is considered...an ambitious man, and therefore a dangerous one. That he is ambitious I shall readily grant, but it is of that laudable kind which prompts a man to excel in whatever he takes in hand." That kind of republicanism, the belief that "the spur of fame" disciplines as well as energizes leaders carrying the heaviest burdens, came from Roman republican sources. The War for Independence and the drafting and ratification of the Constitution drew upon, and vindicated, leaders who asked that merited fame be the test of their service to the people.

The same republican heritage that motivated Hamilton and Washington to cultivate ancient virtues caused other republicans to draw back from the exercise of power and view its exercise with distaste and apprehension. They harkened most readily to Roman virtues of simplicity and frugality and to Harrington's view that independent landowners alone had the prerequisites for virtuous political conduct. The tenacity with which Jeffersonian republicans opposed Hamilton's policies—especially the Jay Treaty of 1795, which restored normal relations with Great Britain—had deep roots in classical republican ideology and also American opposition politics.

In *The Jeffersonian Persuasion: Evolution of a Party Ideology* (1978), Lance Banning examined the grip of the past—the hold of the country ideology on American political behavior. He begins with the antifederalists, who found a home in the Republican party. Although Madison believed that he had answered their arguments about factionalism and the abuse of power in *The Federalist*, Banning locates two serious concerns on which they remained unmollified. The antifederalists found the mixed government provisions of the Constitution deficient because the House of Representatives was too small a body, with members representing populous districts, to mirror the people. And they predicted that the indirect election of both the Senate and the President would cause the two to coalesce into a single aristocratic branch of government. But the antifederalists accepted the Constitution, once it had been ratified, in order to mitigate these weaknesses and resist the corruption of public life they feared was coming.

During the late 1790s, Hamilton's followers, now organized as the Federalist party, whipped up anti-French hysteria as a means of discrediting Jefferson's and Madison's opposition Republican party. An anguished President John Adams saw Hamiltonians in his own cabinet ignore his leadership and mock his desire to see the presidency function as a nonpartisan balance above contending groups. Virginia Republicans saw liberty itself jeopardized by partisan measures like the Alien and Sedition Acts and the creation of an army, ostensibly to repel French invasion but more likely to intimidate the opposition. Republicans enunciated in 1798 principles of limited government that successive generations of southern conservatives cherished as "the principles of '98." Pointing with alarm at "uncontrolled power," "treasures of corruption" distributed among "devoted partisans," and at the "dexterity which ambition never fails to display," the Virginia Republicans prepared to do battle in the 1800 election for control of the national government.

When they won that election, Jefferson and his party were both burdened and empowered by their English country party ideology. Jefferson acted moderately to dismantle some features of Federalist rule and to maintain, for the time being, Hamilton's fiscal reforms that could not be safely or easily scuttled. But even allowing for such political sagacity, Jeffersonians in power remained truer to their ideological heritage than have most successful movements in American history. They truly believed, in principle if not always in practice, as Banning succinctly writes, "that power was a monster, and governing was wrong."

Both the Jeffersonian suspicion of power and the Hamiltonian appreciation of its uses were rooted in republican ideology. The cause of continuing partisanship from 1793 to 1815 was the determination of both parties to "secure the Revolution"—that is, to prevent each other from squandering the legacy of republican government for which the Revolution had been fought. When Jefferson told the nation in 1801, "we are all republicans; we are all federalists," he meant that the struggle to preserve the Revolutionary legacy was both divisive and healing, and he sought to make this paradox into a creative maxim of government:

> I know...that some men fear that a republican government cannot be strong, that this government is not strong enough. But would the honest patriot, in the full tide of a successful experiment, abandon a government which has so far kept us free and firm, on the theoretic and visionary fear that this government...may...want the energy to preserve itself? I trust not.... I believe this...government...is the only one...on earth...where every man...would meet invasions of the public order as his own personal concern.

Ultimately, the choice between theoretical fears and firm accomplishments was, as Jefferson said, a matter of "trust":

> Sometimes it is said that man cannot be trusted with the government of himself. Can he then be trusted with the government of others? Or have we found angels in the form of kings to govern him. Let history answer this question.

As this book has shown, history has answered the question affirmatively. Human beings are capable of self-government. But that answer is also a lesson that can be forgotten and misapplied. When elements of the historical record like moral discourse, political ethics, the high seriousness of civic life—in a word, ideology—are forgotten and slip from the historical record, the intellectual effort required to restore that record is Herculean.

With only a few exceptions, conservatives and liberals in contemporary America have little sense of history. The example of conservatives like Burke, Calhoun, Disraeli, Taft, or Churchill rarely stir the imaginations of conservative politicians today, and unlike New Deal politicians of a generation ago, today's liberals exhibit little familiarity with their Jeffersonian, Jacksonian, and progressive forebears. The immense debt of both liberalism and conservatism to Locke or to John Stuart Mill, the nineteenth-century theorist of liberalism, has been virtually forgotten by politically conscious Americans.

As the historical and philosophical content of political discourse has become shallow and debased, so the persuasiveness of political arguments has suffered. Uncomfortable with ideas and given more to posturing than to reasoned and reasonable argument, American political leaders—with a few notable exceptions—have little of Madison's instinct for common ground, Jefferson's ability to fashion rational ideals into political solutions, or Hamilton's interest in channeling human nature into constructive public policies. Recovering our ability to do battle over ideas ought to begin with a thoughtful revisiting of the ideological battles of the seventeenth and eighteenth centuries that created the American republic.

Afterword

BETWEEN 1965, when Bailyn published his edition of Revolutionary pamphlets, and 1986, when Lance Banning and Joyce Appleby debated republican ideology in the *William and Mary Quarterly*, differences of interpretation have first widened and then narrowed. They widened from the late 1960s to the mid-1970s as Pocock, Wood, and Banning put forth a more exclusively *republican* version of the ideological interpretation and as Jack P. Greene, Isaac Kramnick, John P. Diggins, and Joyce Appleby countered that a *liberal* tradition of Lockean natural and individual rights was just as important ideologically as republican opposition thought. They narrowed between the mid-1970s and early 1990s as James T. Kloppenberg, Forrest McDonald, Peter Onuf, and Richard C. Sinopoli found ways to reconcile republican and liberal understandings.

Most historians now agree on four important points. First, they accept that the ideology of the Revolution was both republican and Lockean. Second, they agree that compact theory sanctioned personal freedom while republicanism functioned best as a diagnosis of the threat that tyranny posed to the community. Third, historians realize that the patriots drew eclectically on both Lockean and republican ideas and ignored, or were oblivious to, the incompatibility of the two traditions. Fourth, historians concur that Scottish republicanism—the Aristotelian civic foundations of Common Sense moral philosophy—was more compatible with Lockean political philosophy than was the English country ideology and that Scottish ideas gained decidedly in influence by the time of the drafting and ratification of the Constitution.

As Kloppenberg explains in an insightful evaluation of the republicanism controversy, the Revolutionary era represents a rare and fleeting convergence of Renaissance, civic humanist ideals of dutiful citizenship and Lockean natural-right defense of freedom. "American revolutionaries," Kloppenberg concludes, "committed themselves to a pair of principles that held a formidable challenge to the new nation."

The tensions within republicanism—as well as those between the Lockean and republican heritages—produced in the first half of the nineteenth century sharply divergent political philosophies. The clash between republican jealousy and republican national consolidation, which surfaced between the 1770s and the 1790s, was symptomatic of troubles to come.

Republicanism inspired an indigenous democratic radicalism among artisans and craftsmen in the half century following the Revolution, described most fully in Sean Wilentz, *Chants Democratic: New York City and the Rise of the American Working Class, 1788–1785* (1984). Wilentz acknowledges the strong individualism, marketplace enterprise, and "bourgeois propriety" of these people. "Yet the mechanics, with their artisan republicanism," Wilentz insists, "also stood for much more. With a rhetoric rich in the republican language of corruption, equality, and independence, they remained committed to a benevolent hierarchy of skill and the co-operative workshop,...a moral order in which all craftsmen would eventually become self-governing, independent, competent masters." John L. Brooke finds the same kind of egalitarian republicanism in Worcester County, Massachusetts. Amos Singletary had electrified the Massachusetts ratification convention in 1788 when he accused "lawyers, and men of learning, and moneyed men who talk so finely" of trying to hoodwink "us poor, illiterate people" into swallowing the proposed federal Constitution so that they "would get all the power and all the money into their own hands." As for many Revolutionary republicans at the local level, religion and politics were closely interwoven for Singletary. A staunch Congregationalist, he was taunted by a Baptist blacksmith, "O squire! O squire! What shall I do to be saved?" Singletary reportedly shot back with a characteristically republican moral rebuke: "Put more steel in your hoes."

Indeed, religion played a critical role in the popularization of republicanism. In *The Democratization of American Christianity*, Nathan O. Hatch locates a wide range of experimental, unlettered, spontaneous religious movements that "empowered ordinary people to take their own deepest spiritual impulses at face value"; these included Baptist, Methodist, African-American, and Mormon churches that destabilized elite leadership in American religious life and discredited formal learning, which was the exclusive possession of men with college and seminary degrees and training in ancient languages.

Republicanism also facilitated the very kind of change that Amos Singletary feared and detested. In the hands of the first generation of post-Revolutionary lawyers and judges, court decisions undermined the use of the English common law as a protection of landed property and created instead what Morton J. Horwitz calls "an instrumental conception of law, ... providing for the subsidization of enterprise and permitting the legal destruction of old forms of property for the benefit of more recent entrants." Thus courts allowed the damming and diversion of rivers and streams in the interests of producing water power and the building of railroads over the objections of landowners inconvenienced and even harmed by the new technology. James Henretta associates this transformation of the law with Lockean individualism among the legal and commercial elite, who saw community constraints on business enterprise as an anachronistic republican holdover from the eighteenth century.

Supreme Court Justice Joseph Story (1779–1845) devoted his long career as a jurist and legal scholar to harmonizing and systematizing conservative republican and Lockean jurisprudence. Along with John Quincy Adams, Story was an early New England recruit in Jefferson's Republican party, and he considered the New England Federalists to be excessively hierarchical and rigid. In place of Federalist partisanship, Story wanted to blend Enlightenment scrutiny of society and institutions, Adam Smith's marketplace economics, John Locke's natural rights, and Edmund Burke's vision of heroic political leadership. As Story's biographer, R. Kent Newmyer, writes: "Story would unleash the creative energies of individuals through commercial and constitutional law on the assumption that national union would thereby be strengthened.... Like the authors of the *Federalist*, Story saw law as an instrument by which men institutionalized their rational moments as a bulwark against foolishness, passions, and selfishness." That was the essence of his republicanism.

Republicanism also became deeply reactionary. When John C. Calhoun rose in the Senate in 1833 to denounce the Force Bill for the collection of federal import duties in spite of South Carolina's nullification of the tariff of 1828, he reviewed both the Lockean and republican traditions that South Carolinians, indeed all Americans, had cherished since 1776. Until that point in his career, Calhoun had been a Lockean who supported the Constitution as a compact between the people and their government (or as he would now insist, the states and the national government). The compact made American statesmen into a fraternity of high-minded gentlemen who mutually respected and trusted one another. But the growing power of economic interest groups braying at Congress for special favors and the alarming rise of abolitionist demagoguery now convinced Calhoun that the optimistic and rational methods of Lockean liberalism could no longer protect South Carolina's liberty. A crisis of political survival had arrived, and the people of South Carolina, and perhaps all of the slave-owning South, would have to adopt intransigent opposition to further incursions of federal authority. The issue rested, Calhoun said, in the hands of "a mysterious Providence." He did not employ that concept as a religious one nearly so much as he made it an ideological republican phrase. For Calhoun, a mysterious Providence resembled Machiavelli's concept of *fortuna*—all the misfortunes that can befall a state regardless of the skill and foresight of its rulers and the virtue and discipline of its people. The defense of slavery became increasingly a republican effort to preserve virtue, independence, and autonomy within the slave system. Yet, as Garry Wills has recently shown, classical republican values permeated Lincoln's great funeral oration on equality at Gettysburg in 1863.

Americans won their independence and built their new constitutional government on republican, as well as Lockean, foundations. But they made the most of the elasticity of their republican-Lockean heritage. Stretching it to uphold freedom and slavery, equality and social cohesion, individualism and human solidarity, nineteenth-century Americans finally made these great seventeenth- and eighteenth-century ideas artifacts of a glorious libertarian and revolutionary past.

Artifacts they might have remained but for two developments. First, as this book has shown, historians during the 1960s and 1970s discovered Revolutionary ideology. Second, political theorists during the 1980s and early 1990s have begun to search for historic values that can hold the American polity together in a new, post-industrial age of racial, ethnic, religious, generational, and economic conflict that threatens the very stability of the republic. In *The Reinterpretation of American Citizenship: Liberalism, the Constitution, and Civic Virtue* (1992), Richard Sinopoli examines the framers' expectations about citizen involvement in American public life under the Constitution. The "most valuable and still most viable" element in the "founders' politics," he writes, was their "commitment to liberal justice that recognizes the moral worth of each person and embodies it politically in a commitment to fundamental rights." The framers assumed that individuals were conscious of their own dignity and valued—as much as virtue itself—their own autonomy. Individually, persons free to pursue their own interests could also be expected to balance their self-interest against their duty to the community. But the reverse—that public-spirited citizens will automatically "balance the competing demands of civic and private life"—is by no means axiomatic or assured. The framers doubted whether "active patriotism" of the kind displayed in the Revolutionary War was "sustained in periods of normal politics."

Sinopoli contends that the Constitution was intended to inculcate civic-mindedness in the populace by capitalizing on virtues that grew out of self-interest—industry from ambition, for one example, or trust from gratitude for another. By rewarding industry, government could convert raw ambition into socially redemptive behavior; by making elected officials grateful to their constituents, the elective process could seal the bond between the people and their government. The experience of the framers suggests that complex moral choices cannot be made democratically by the people, but that governments and politicians have a vested interest in absorbing into public policy as much as possible of the moral convictions of members of the populace as a means of bonding the people to their own government.

Bibliographical Essay

ALTHOUGH this book does not have footnotes, each title in the Bibliographical Essay appears in the same sequence as do quotations, major interpretations, and points of fact in the text.

Ideology as a Way of Thinking about the American Revolution

For a comprehensive collection of interpretive essays about the various aspects of the Revolution, see Jack P. Greene and J. R. Pole, eds., *The Blackwell Encyclopedia of the American Revolution* (1991). An excellent example of the Revolution as a political crisis at the local level is the downfall of the "River Gods" in western Massachusetts. The details of one revealing episode are in Robert M. Calhoon, *The Loyalists in Revolutionary America, 1760–1781* (1973), and the larger context is reconstructed in Gregory N. Nobles, *Divisions throughout the Whole: Politics and Society in Hampshire County, Massachusetts* (1983). Other valuable accounts include Robert J. Taylor, *Western Massachusetts in the Revolution* (1954) Robert Zemsky, *Merchants, Farmers, and River Gods: An Essay on Eighteenth-Century American Politics* (1971), and Franklin B. Dexter, *Biographical Sketches of Graduates of Yale College*, Volume 2 (1895).

Andrew C. McLaughlin, *The Foundations of American Constitutionalism* (1932) remains the foundation for the study of constitutional conflict in the Revolution. Jack P. Greene, *Peripheries and Center: Constitutional Development of the Extended Polities of the British Empire and the United States, 1607–1788* (1986) is the best recent account. Greene's article, "Bridge to Revolution: The Wilkes Fund Controversy in South Carolina," *Journal of Southern History* (1963) is the standard account of that dispute, and it is set further in context in Greene's edition of *The Nature of Colony Constitutions: Two Pamphlets on the Wilkes Fund Controversy in South Carolina by Egerton Leigh and Arthur Lee* (1970) and his book, *The Quest for Power: The Lower Houses of Assembly in the Southern Royal Colonies* (1963).

The economic stresses in the British Empire are examined in John J. McCusker and Russell R. Menard, *The Economy of British America, 1607–1789* (1985). For the Boston Tea Party, see Benjamin Labaree, *The Boston Tea Party* (1964), John W. Tyler, *Smugglers & Patriots: Boston Merchants and the Advent of the Revolution* (1986), P. D. G. Thomas, *The Townshend Duties Crisis: The Second Phase of the American Revolution, 1767–1773* (1987), and Richard B. Sheridan, "The British Credit Crisis of 1772 and the American Colonies," *Journal of Economic History* (1960).

Social stress in Revolutionary Virginia is the dramatic climax of Gordon S. Wood, "Rhetoric and Reality in the American Revolution," *William and Mary Quarterly* (1966), though Carl Bridenbaugh independently made the same discovery in "Violence and Virtue in Virginia, 1766: Or the Importance of the Trivial," *Proceedings* of the Massachusetts Historical Society (1964), reprinted in Bridenbaugh, *Early Americans* (1981). Two essays by Jack P. Greene treat this stress as cultural and moral rather than social: "Character, Persona, and Authority: A Study of Alternative Styles of Political Leadership in Revolutionary Virginia," W. Robert Higgins, ed., *The Revolutionary War in the South: Power, Conflict, and Leadership* (1979) and "'*Virtus et Libertas*': Political Culture, Social Change, and the Origins of the American Revolution in Virginia, 1763–1776," Jeffrey J. Crow and Larry E. Tise, eds., *The Southern Experience in the American Revolution* (1978). T. H. Breen, *Tobacco Culture: The Mentality of the Great Tidewater Planters on the Eve of Revolution* (1985) combines social and cultural analysis while Rhys Isaac, *The Transformation of Virginia, 1740–1790* (1982) pits planter aristocrats against evangelical yeoman farmers. Gerald W. Mullin, *Flight and Rebellion: Slave Resistance in Eighteenth-Century Virginia* (1972) discovers acculturation of skilled slaves as a strategy for making slavery less barbarous and an opportunity for a black elite to resist bondage, and Edmund S. Morgan, *American Slavery/American Freedom: The Ordeal of Colonial Virginia* (1975) reinterprets the moral, political, and social effect of slave owning on Virginia whites.

George Lichtheim, *The Concept of Ideology and Other Essays* (1967) locates the origin of the term *ideology* in the French Revolution. In 1795, the Institute of France—a sort of "think tank" created by the National Convention to realize Condorcet's vision of progress through intellectual inquiry—identified as "ideologues" the moderate liberals of the French Revolution who upheld the liberty of the mind but accepted temporary despotism as the price of social order. That first ideology resembled the beliefs of Alexander Hamilton and other high Federalists in the United States during the late 1790s. For a comparative study of the two revolutions, which stresses the centrality of such moderate liberalism in America and France, see Patrice Higonnet, *Sister Republics: The Origins of French and American Republicanism* (1988).

The ideological interpretation of the American Revolution is evaluated in Robert E. Shalhope, "Toward a Republican Synthesis: The Emergence of an Understanding of Republicanism in American Historiography" and "Republicanism and Early American Historiography," both in the *William and Mary Quarterly* (1972, 1982 respectively). See also Gordon S. Wood, "Ideology and the Origins of Liberal America," Lance Banning, "Jeffersonian Ideology Revisited: Liberal and Classical Ideas in the New American Republic," also in the *William and Mary Quarterly* (1987 and 1986 respectively), and Joyce Appleby, *Liberalism and Republicanism in Historical Imagination* (1992). In addition to Bailyn's *Pamphlets* and *Ideological Origins*, his *The Origin of American Politics* (1968) explores colonial receptiveness to English opposition ideas. On Bolingbroke and changing colonial attitudes toward monarchy, see William D. Liddle, "'A Patriot King, or None': Lord Bolingbroke and the American Renunciation of George III," *Journal of American History* (1979) and Gordon S. Wood, *The Radicalism of the American Revolution* (1992). On the way songs spread republicanism, see Arthur Shrader, *American Revolutionary War Songs to Cultivate the Sensations of Liberty*, Folkways Records (1976), which includes superb scholarly notes.

On historians as a guild and as participants in their culture, see

Peter Novick, *That Noble Dream: The "Objectivity Question" and the American Historical Profession* (1988) and David A. Hollinger, *In the American Province* (1985). Quentin Skinner has been a particularly influential writer on political thought during the early modern period; James Tully, ed., *Meaning and Context: Quentin Skinner and his Critics* (1988) is a convenient source on this methodology. See also James T. Kloppenberg, "The Virtues of Liberalism: Christianity, Republicanism, and Ethics in Early American Discourse," *Journal of American History* (1987).

Edward Shils, *Center and Periphery: Essays on Macrosociology* (1975) defines the concept, and Ernest Gellner, "Ethnicity Unbound," *New Republic* (June 18, 1990) is an excellent criticism of the uses historians and political scientists have made of the center-periphery model.

On the pioneers of ideological history, see: on Mannheim, Henk W. S. Woldring, *Karl Mannheim* (1986); on Geertz, see his "Thick Description: Toward an Interpretive Theory of Culture" in Geertz, *The Interpretation of Culture* (1975) and Joyce Appleby, "Value and Society," in Jack P. Greene and J. R. Pole, eds., *Colonial British America: Essays in the New History of the Early Modern Era* (1984); on Robbins, see her "Douglass Adair: A Personal Memoir," in Trevor Colbourn, ed., *Fame and the Founding Fathers: Essays of Douglass Adair* (1974); on Pocock, see J. H. Hexter, *On Historians* (1979); on Palmer, see his "Generalizations about Revolution: A Case Study," in Louis R. Gottschalk, ed., *Generalization in the Writing of History* (1963); on the new rhetoric, see James T. Boulton, *The Language of Politics in the Age of Wilkes and Paine* (1963) and David A. Wilson, *Paine and Cobbett: The Trans-Atlantic Connection* (1988); on political culture, see Lucian W. Pye and Sidney Verba, eds., *Political Culture and Political Development* (1965).

The English Philosophy of Order, 1660–1714

The tradition of order in seventeenth-century English politics is treated in W. H. Greenleaf, *Order, Empiricism, and Politics.* Augmenting Greenleaf is David Armitage, "The Cromwellian Protectorate and the Language of Empires," *Historical Journal* (1992). J. R. Pole, *The Gift of Government: Political Responsibility from the English Restoration to American Independence* (1983) links Restoration politics to the American Revolution and, as its title suggests, considers the lessons learned from the 1660–1776 period a profoundly fortunate circumstance in history. Greene, *Peripheries and Center* and his "Political Mimesis: A Consideration of the British Colonies in the Eighteenth Century," *American Historical Review* (1969) argues that royal authority in the Restoration Empire was improvised and vulnerable to unsettling contingencies. In contrast with Pole and with Greene, Stephen Saunders Webb, *The Governors-General: The English Army and the Definition of the Empire, 1569–1681* (1979) and *1676: The End of American Independence* (1984) and David Hackett Fischer, *Albion's Seed: Four British Folkways in America* (1989) find a hegemonic Restoration regime that persisted long into the eighteenth century.

Three volumes in the *History of the American Colonies* series edited by Milton M. Klein and Jacob E. Cooke treat Proprietary politics with great insight and originality: Michael Kammen, *Colonial New York: A History* (1975), Joseph E. Illick, *Colonial Pennsylvania: A History* (1976), and Robert M. Weir, *Colonial South Carolina: A History* (1983). On Harrington, see J. G. A. Pocock, ed., *The Political Works of James Harrington* (1977) and H. F. Russell Smith, *Harrington and his Oceana* (1914). On Hobbes, see James R. Stoner, *Common Law and Liberal Theory: Coke, Hobbes, and the Origins of American Constitutionalism* (1992).

For the Glorious Revolution in England and America, see J. R. Jones, *The Revolution of 1688 in England* (1973), Lois Schwoerer, *The Declaration of Rights, 1689* (1981), Edmund S. Morgan, *Inventing the People: The Rise of Popular Sovereignty in England and America* (1988), and David S. Lovejoy, *The Glorious Revolution in America* (1972). On Locke, see Peter Laslett, ed., *Two Treatises of Government* (1952), John Dunn, *Political Obligation in its Historical Context: Essays in Political Theory* (1980), and Richard Ashcraft, *Revolutionary Politics & Locke's Two Treatises of Government* (1986). Thomas L. Pangle, *The Spirit of Modern Republicanism: The Moral Vision of the American Founders and the Philosophy of Locke* (1988) argues strenuously for the similarity of Locke and the Commonwealth tradition. Gerald M. Straka, *Anglican Reaction to the Revolution of 1688* (1962), Norman Sykes, *Church and State in England in the Eighteenth Century* (1934), and Geoffrey Holmes, *The Trial of Dr. Sacheverell* (1973) explore the political involvements of the Anglican Church.

The Anglican mission to America is introduced authoritatively in

John C. Van Horne, ed., *Religious Philanthropy and Colonial Slavery: The American Correspondence of the Associates of Dr. Bray, 1717–1777* (1985) and in John Calam, *Parsons and Pedagogues: The S.P.G. Adventure in American Education* (1971). The cultural significance of Anglicanism in America is one of the many concerns of the brilliant exploratory study, Jon Butler, *Awash in a Sea of Faith: Christianizing the American People* (1990), in which the author makes very good use of two primary sources edited by Frank J. Klingberg: the sermons preached at the annual meetings of the S.P.G. in 1711, 1741, and 1766 respectively, as an appendix to *Anglican Humanitarianism in Colonial New York* (1940) and *The Carolina Chronicle of Dr. Francis Le Jau, 1706–1717* (1956). Joseph J. Ellis, *The New England Mind in Transition: Samuel Johnson of Connecticut* (1973) examines the major figure in colonial Anglicanism, and Johnson's treatise on "Raphael or the Genius of English America, a Rhapsody" is printed in Herbert and Carol Johnson, eds., *Samuel Johnson: His Career and Writings*, Volume 2 (1929).

A Mature Metropolitan System and its Social Costs, 1714–1773

The foundation for understanding the Whig Supremacy that came to dominate British politics in the decade following the Hanoverian succession is J. H. Plumb, *Sir Robert Walpole: The Making of a Statesman* (1956, 1961) and *The Origins of Political Stability, England, 1675–1725*. James A. Henretta, *"Salutary Neglect": Colonial Administration under the Duke of Newcastle* (1972) details the use of the imperial bureaucracy to stabilize the Whig supremacy. John Brewer, *The Sinews of Power: War, Money, and the English State, 1688–1783* (1989) extends this thesis to the century from the Glorious Revolution to the close of the American War for Independence.

Four documents that illustrate the mindsets of imperial administrators and their ministerial overlords are Martin Bladen and others to the King, Sept. 8, 1721, in Edmund B. O'Callahan, ed., *Documents Relative to the Colonial History of New York* Volume 5 (1855), Jack P. Greene, ed., "William Knox's Explanation for the American Revolution," *William and Mary Quarterly* (1973), Charles Delafaye to Francis Nicholson, Jan. 26, 1722, in Jack P. Greene, ed., *Settlements to*

Society (1966), and Jack P Greene, ed., "The Case of the Pistole Fee: A Report of a Hearing on the Pistole Fee Dispute before the Privy Council, June 18, 1754," *Virginia Magazine of History and Biography* (1958). The identification of Benjamin Godin as subject of the letter to Nicholson is based on evidence in Walter B. Edgar and N. Louise Bailey, eds., *Biographical Dictionary of the South Carolina House of Representatives: The Common House of Assembly, 1692–1775* (1977).

The classic account of Trenchard and Gordon is in Robbins, *Eighteenth-Century Commonwealthman*, but it should be qualified by Ronald Hamowy's article, "Cato's Letters, John Locke, and the Republican Paradigm," in the journal, *History of Political Thought* (1990). See also Marie P. McMahon, *The Radical Whigs, John Trenchard and Thomas Gordon: Libertarian Loyalists to the New House of Hanover* (1990). On Algernon Sidney, see Jonathan Scott, *Algernon Sidney and the Restoration Crisis, 1677–1683* (1991) and Alan Craig Houston, *Algernon Sidney and the Republican Heritage in England and America.* Bailyn, *Ideological Origins*, Robbins, *Commonwealthman*, and Sykes, *Church and State in England* all treat Hoadly. Isaac Kramnick, *Bolingbroke and his Circle: The Politics of Nostalgia in the Age of Walpole* (1968) is the most original and penetrating study of Bolingbroke. On the patriot king concept, see Liddle, "A Patriot King, or None...."

On Hume and the Scottish moral philosophers, see Robbins, *Commonwealthman* and Richard B. Sher and Jeffrey R. Smitten, eds., *Scotland and American in the Age of Enlightenment* (1990). Morgan, *Inventing the People* discovered Hume's theory about the power of "opinion" in government, and Douglass Adair found Hume's concept of extended republics, see Colbourn, ed., *Fame and the Founding Fathers.* Hutcheson's views on colonial independence are quoted in Caroline Robbins, "'When It Is that Colonies May Turn Independent': An Analysis of the Environment and Politics of Francis Hutcheson (1694–1746)," *William and Mary Quarterly* (1957). The best brief analysis of Adam Smith's moral philosophy and political economy is in Robert Heilbroner, ed., *The Essential Adam Smith* (1968). For Hutcheson's and Witherspoon's influence on James Madison, see Robert M. Calhoon, *Evangelicals and Conservatives in the Early South, 1740–1861* (1988) and Douglas Sloan, *The Scottish Enlightenment and the American College Ideal* (1971).

George Rude, *Wilkes and Liberty: A Social Study of 1763 to 1764* (1962) and Ian R. Christie, *Wilkes, Wyvill, and Reform: The Parliamentary Reform Movement in British Politics, 1760–1785* (1962) place Wilkes in context. Isaac Kramnick's essay, "James Burgh and 'Opposition' Ideology in England and America" in *Republicanism and Bourgeoisie Radicalism: Political Ideology in Late Eighteenth-Century England and America* (1990) both acknowledges Burgh's Commonwealth credentials and identifies his Lockean moralism.

Michael Kammen, *A Rope of Sand: The Colonial Agents, Politics, and the American Revolution* (1968) throws much light on Burke's involvement in American affairs. Harvey Mansfield, Jr., *Statesmanship and Party Government: A Study of Burke and Bolingbroke* (1965) analyzes Burke's concept of party. Carl Cone, *Burke and the Nature of Politics: The Age of the American Revolution* (1957) is a basic account. Calhoon, *Evangelicals and Conservatives* discusses the uses Americans made of Burke. On the British bureaucracy on the eve of the Revolution, see Dora Mae Clark, *The Rise of the British Treasury* (1960), Thomas C. Barrow, *Trade and Empire: The British Customs Service in Colonial America, 1660–1775* (1967), and Franklin W. Wickwire, *British Subministers and Colonial America, 1763–1783* (1966).

John Phillip Reid, *The Constitutional History of the American Revolution* (1986, 1987, 1991) identifies distinct imperial and colonial constitutions and theories of legal rights, and Greene, *Peripheries and Center*, discusses the significance of the new legal history of the Revolution.

Ideology and Character in the Revolutionary Crisis, 1774–1776

The best portrait of John Adams is in Bernard Bailyn, *Faces of Revolution: Personalities and Themes in the Struggle for American Independence* (1990), though the original version of this essay, "Butterfield's Adams: Notes for a Sketch" (*William and Mary Quarterly*, 1962) offers a more idiosyncratic and arresting justification for an analysis of Adams's character. John R. Howe, *The Changing Political Thought of John Adams* (1966) and Peter Shaw, *The Character of John Adams* (1976) are also indispensable. Forrest McDonald, *The Presidency of George Washington* (1974) contains astute judgments on Adams,

Hamilton, and Washington, as does Albert Furtwangler, *American Silhouettes: Rhetorical Identities of the Founders* (1987). Robert J. Taylor, ed., *Papers of John Adams*, Volume 4 (1979) publishes the successive drafts of *Thoughts on Government*. J. W. Gough, *John Locke's Political Philosophy: Eight Studies* (1973) is essential for understanding Adams's use of Locke in *Thoughts*.

Mary Beth Norton, *Liberty's Daughters: The Revolutionary Experience of American Women, 1750–1800* (1980) and Linda K. Kerber, *Women of the Republic: Intellect and Ideology in Revolutionary America* (1980) are the basic works on ideology and gender. The division of loyalist ideology into categories of principle, accommodation, and doctrine is from Calhoon, *The Loyalists in Revolutionary America* and, in shorter form, from the title essay of *The Loyalist Perception and Other Essays* (1989). These accounts should be compared with L. F. S. Upton, "The Dilemma of the Loyalist Pamphleteers," *Studies in Burke and his Time* (1977), which emphasizes the Augustan English conservative roots of loyalist ideology, Jeffrey M. Nelson, "Ideology in Search of a Context: Eighteenth-Century British Political Thought and the Loyalists of the American Revolution," *Historical Journal* (1977), which correctly emphasizes the importance of statute law for the loyalists, and Janice Potter, *The Liberty We Seek: Loyalist Ideology in Colonial New York and Massachusetts* (1983), which conflates the categories of principle and doctrine. Bailyn, *Ideological Origins* has a brilliant passage on Thomas Bradbury Chandler. Anne Young Zimmer, *Jonathan Boucher: Loyalist in Exile* (1978) suggests that Boucher added Filmer to his 1775 sermon on obedience prior to the publication of his colonial sermons in 1797 in reaction to the excesses of the French Revolution.

There is a very rich body of scholarship on the Pennsylvania radicals including Gordon S. Wood, *The Creation of the American Republic, 1776–1787* (1969), David Hawke, *In the Midst of a Revolution* (1961), J. R. Pole, *Political Representation in England and the Origins of the American Republic* (1966), Richard Alan Ryerson, *The Revolution is Now Begun: The Radical Committees of Philadelphia, 1765–1776* (1978), Eric Foner, *Tom Paine and Revolutionary America* (1976), and Douglas M. Arnold, *A Republican Revolution: Ideology and Politics in Pennsylvania* (1989). Houston, *Algernon Sidney* relates Benjamin Rush's discovery of Sidney's republicanism.

On Richard Price, see Bernard Peach, ed., *Richard Price and the Ethical Foundations of the American Revolution* (1979). The literature on Jefferson and Revolutionary ideology is, of course, quite extensive. Merrill Peterson, *Thomas Jefferson and the New Nation* (1970) gives an excellent account of the drafting of *Summary View*. Peterson's *Adams and Jefferson: A Revolutionary Dialogue* (1976) explores that famous intellectual friendship. Trevor Colbourn, *The Lamp of Experience: Whig History and the Intellectual Origins of the American Revolution* (1965) reconstructs Jefferson's complex understanding of history. Sheldon, *Political Philosophy of Thomas Jefferson* expertly incorporates prior scholarship into a careful textual reading of Jefferson. Wilbur S. Howell, "The Declaration of Independence and Eighteenth-Century Logic," *William and Mary Quarterly* (1961) established Jefferson's debt to the Scottish rhetorician, William Duncan. Colbourn, ed., *Fame and the Founding Fathers* contains Adair's essay on Jefferson and Count Rumdold. See also Peter Onuf, ed., *Jeffersonian Legacies* (1993) and Jay Fliegelman, *Declaring Independence: Jefferson, Natural Language, and the Culture of Performance* (1993).

For a wide-ranging study of these issues, see Jack P. Greene, *Imperatives, Behaviors, & Identities: Essays in Early American Cultural History* (1992). Other studies of the role of ideology in the Revolutionary crisis of 1774–1776 include Pauline Maier, *From Resistance to Revolution: Colonial Radicals and the Development of American Opposition to Britain, 1765–1776* (1972) and *The Old Revolutionaries: Political Lives in the Age of Samuel Adams* (1980), Robert M. Weir, *"The Last of American Freemen": Studies in the Political Culture of the Colonial and Revolutionary South* (1986) and Weir, ed., *The Letters of Freeman, Etc.: Essays on the Non-Importation Movement in South Carolina Collected by William Henry Drayton* (1977), Bernard Bailyn, *The Ordeal of Thomas Hutchinson* (1974), William Pencak, *America's Burke: The Mind of Thomas Hutchinson* (1982), Richard Bushman, *King and People in Provincial Massachusetts* (1985), James H. Kettner, *The Development of American Citizenship, 1607–1870* (1978), Jerrilyn Greene Marston, *King and Congress: The Transfer of Political Legitimacy, 1774–1776* (1987), and Jack N. Rakove, *The Beginnings of National Politics: An Interpretive History of the Continental Congress* (1979). For an earlier formulation of this interpretation, see Robert M. Calhoon, *Revolutionary America: An Interpretive Overview* (1976).

Revolutionary War and the Sources of Conflict in American Society, 1776–1783

The social analysis of the Revolutionary War is the subject of two luminous volumes of essays by the two foremost historians of the military history of the Revolution, John Shy, *A People Numerous and Armed* (1976, revised 1990) and Don Higginbotham, *War and Society in Revolutionary America: The Wider Dimensions of Conflict* (1988). The best soldiers' songs of the War are recorded and superbly annotated in Arthur F. Shrader, *Songs to Cultivate the Sensations of Freedom.* Germain's approach to the Revolutionary War is examined sympathetically in Gerald Saxon Brown, *The American Secretary: The Colonial Policy of Lord George Germain, 1775–1778* (1963) and more critically in Ira D. Gruber, *The Howe Brothers and the American Revolution* (1972). The ethnic, racial, and social divisions enflamed by armed hostilities are described in Calhoon, *The Loyalists in Revolutionary America* and *The Loyalist Perception and Other Essays*, accounts based in part on Benjamin Quarles, *The Negro in the American Revolution* (1961), Adrian C. Leiby, *The Revolutionary War in the Hackensack Valley: The Jersey Dutch and the Neutral Ground* (1962), Barbara Graymont, *The Iroquois and the American Revolution* (1972), James H. O'Donnell, *Southern Indians in the American Revolution* (1973), and J. Leitch Wright, *Britain and the American Frontier, 1783–1815* (1975). The first book on Indians to connect their conduct in the Revolutionary War to their religious beliefs is Dowd, *A Spiritual Resistance.* See also Edward J. Cashin, *The King's Ranger* (1989). Bernard W. Sheehan, *Seeds of Extinction: Jeffersonian Philanthropy and the American Indian* (1973) examines Jefferson's hopes for the Americanization of the Indians.

Donald L. Robinson, *Slavery in the Structure of American Politics, 1765–1820* (1971) is a thorough study and Duncan McLeod, *Slavery, Race, and the American Revolution* (1974) is a provocative intellectual history of the subject. They are now joined by Sylvia R. Frey, *Water from the Rock: Black Resistance in a Revolutionary Age* (1991), which teases new evidence from the historical record. "A Few Anonymous Remarks on Lord Dunmore's Proclamation," in Robert L. Schreiner and Brent Tarter, eds., *Revolutionary Virginia: The Road to Independence*, Volume 4 (1978) and Fredrika Teute Schmidt and Barbara Ripel

Wilhelm, "Early Proslavery Petitions in Virginia," *William and Mary Quarterly* (1973) are valuable sources on white reaction to black activism. Robert M. Weir, "*The Last of American Freemen*" has a chapter on John Laurens, whose letters can be found in David Chestnutt, ed. *The Papers of Henry Laurens*, Vols. 12 and 13 (1990, 1992). The best source on Edward Coles's antislavery is Ralph L. Ketcham, "The Dictates of Conscience: Edward Coles and Slavery," *Virginia Quarterly Review* (1960). William W. Freehling, "The Founding Fathers and Slavery," *American Historical Review* (1972) and *The Road to Disunion: Secessionists at Bay, 1776–1854* (1990) make the case for Jefferson's racial statesmanship. The magisterial works on race and the Revolution are Winthrop D. Jordan, *White over Black: American Attitudes Toward the Negro, 1550–1812* (1968) and David Brion Davis, *The Problem of Slavery in the Age of Revolution, 1770–1823* (1975). The view that inequality in Revolutionary society was a dynamic egalitarian force is gracefully argued in Edmund S. Morgan, *The Challenge of the American Revolution* (1976): "The creed of equality did not give men equality, but invited them to claim it, invited them not to know their place and keep it, but to seek and demand a better place."

The best introduction to the metropolitanism of British commanders is George A. Billias, ed., *George Washington's Opponents* (1969) and the following biographies: John Richard Alden, *General Gage in America* (1948), Ira D. Gruber, *The Howe Brothers and the American Revolution*, William B. Willcox, *Portrait of a General: Sir Henry Clinton in the War for Independence* (1962), and Franklin and Mary Wickwire, *Cornwallis: The American Adventure* (1970). On Guy Carleton, see Paul H. Smith, "Sir Guy Carleton, Peace Negotiations, and the Evacuation of New York," *Canadian Historical Review* (1969).

John Adams's use of Sulla to understand the nature of warfare in a republic threatened with despotism is preserved in Paul H. Smith, ed., *Letters of Delegates to Congress, 1774–1789*, Volume 7 (1981) and his classical moderation is examined in James M. Farrell, "John Adams's *Autobiography*: The Ciceronian Paradigm and the Quest for Fame," *New England Quarterly* (1989) and "'Syren Tully' and the Young John Adams," *Classical Journal* (1992). On Lockean moderation, see Laslett, ed., *Two Treatises of Government*, pp. 373–384. On Calvinist moderation, see Richard B. Sher and Jeffrey R. Smitten, eds., *Scotland and American in the Age of the Enlightenment* (1990) and Mark A. Noll, *Princeton and the Republic, 1768–1822* (1989). Marvin B. Endy,

Jr., "Just War, Holy War, and Millennialism in Revolutionary America," *William and Mary Quarterly* (1985) finds political conformity rather than religious radicalism in patriot sermons. See also "Presbyterians in the American Revolution: A Documentary Account," *Journal of Presbyterian History* (1974), Arthur H. Shaffer, *To Be an American: David Ramsay and the Making of American Consciousness* (1991), and Calhoon, *Evangelicals and Conservatives in the Early South.* George Washington's moderation is brilliantly illuminated in Marcus Cunliffe, *George Washington: Man and Monument* (1958), Garry Wills, *Cincinnatus: George Washington and the Enlightenment: Images of Power in Early America* (1984), Page Smith, *A New Age Now Begins* (1976), Don Higginbotham, *George Washington and the American Military Tradition* (1985), and Edmund S. Morgan, *The Genius of George Washington.* Two surprising books, Charles Royster, *A Revolutionary People at War: The Continental Army and American Character, 1775–1783* (1979) and E. Wayne Carp, *To Starve the Army at Pleasure: Continental Army Administration and American Political Culture, 1775–1783* (1984), find the moderate mindset throughout the enlisted men and officers of the Continental army and the Quartermaster staff, respectively.

On the radicalizing impact of the War for Independence, see Ronald Hoffman and Peter J. Albert, eds., *Arms and Independence: The Military Character of the American Revolution* (1984), James Kirby Martin and Mark Edward Lender, *A Respectable Army: The Military Origins of the Republic 1763–1789* (1982), and Richard Buel, *Dear Liberty: Connecticut's Mobilization for the Revolutionary War* (1980). Ronald Hoffman, *A Spirit of Dissension: Economics, Politics, and the Revolution in Maryland* (1973) and Harold B. Hancock, *The Loyalists of Revolutionary Delaware* (1977) independently discovered the Tory populist subculture of the Delmarva peninsula. Keith Mason, "Localism, Evangelicalism and Loyalism: The Sources of Oppression in the Revolutionary Chesapeake," *Journal of Southern History* (1990) and William H. Williams, *The Garden of American Methodism: The Delmarva Peninsula, 1769–1820* (1984) add important additional insights. Stephen A. Marini, *Radical Sects of Revolutionary New England* (1982) and G. A. Rawlyk, *Ravished by the Spirit: Religious Revivals, Baptists, and Henry Alline* (1984) examine folk cultural rebellion in northern New England.

The radical impact of the southern offensive can be pieced together from Ronald Hoffman, Thad W. Tate, and Peter J. Albert, eds., *An Uncivil War: The Southern Backcountry during the American Revolution* (1985), John S. Pancake, *This Destructive War: The British Campaign in the Carolinas, 1780–1782* (1985), Calhoon, *The Loyalist Perception and Other Essays* and Robert M. Calhoon, "Aedanus Burke and Thomas Burke: Revolutionary Conservatism in the Carolinas," in David R. Chesnutt and Clyde N. Wilson, eds., *The Meaning of South Carolina History: Essays in Honor of George C. Rogers, Jr.* (1991) and in Rakove, *Beginnings of National Politics.* On Madison's use of Pericles and Athenian democracy, see Paul A. Rahe, *Republics Ancient and Modern: Classical Republicanism and the American Revolution* (1992). Peter J. Hinks's forthcoming book on David Walker will substantially enlarge our understanding of race and religion in the post-Revolutionary South. David Brion Davis, *Revolutions: Reflections on American Equality and Foreign Liberations* (1990) will probably prove to be a prescient study.

Revolutionary Constitutionalism and Disciplining Ideological Energy, 1783–1801

J. G. A. Pocock, ed., *Three British Revolutions: 1641, 1688, and 1776* (1980) applied Pocock's Machiavellian Moment hypothesis to Anglo-American politics, and John M. Murrin "The Great Inversion, or Court versus Country: A Comparison of the Revolutionary Settlements in England (1688–1721) and America (1776–1816)" does so explicitly and does not stop at 1816 but carries the argument through the age of Jackson. See also James H. Hutson, "Country, Court, and Constitution: Antifederalism and the Historians," *William and Mary Quarterly* (1981). The spectrum of criticism of Pocock runs from Thomas L. Pangle, *The Spirit of Modern Liberalism: The Moral Vision of the American Founders and the Philosophy of Locke* to Kramnick, *Republicanism and Bourgeois Radicalism* to Greene, *Imperatives, Behaviors, and Identities*, and finally to Appleby, *Liberalism and Republicanism in the Historical Imagination.* Daniel T. Rodgers, "Republicanism: The Career of an Idea," *Journal of American History* (1992) places the whole controversy in context. Richard R. Beeman, "Deference, Republicanism, and the Emergence of Popular Politics in Eighteenth-Century America," *William and Mary Quarterly* (1992) discerns the two-faced quality of democratic and elitist republicanism. Gordon S. Wood, *The Creation of the American Republic* makes the strongest case for the constructiveness of republican jealousy while John C. Meleney, *The Public Life of Aedanus Burke: Revolutionary Republican in Post-Revolutionary South Carolina* (1989) is an excellent case study.

Jackson Turner Main, *Political Parties before the Constitution* divides Revolutionary leaders in the 1780s into "localist" and "cosmopolitan" camps. See also Irwin H. Polishook, *Rhode Island and the Union, 1774–1795* (1969), Richard D. Brown, "Shays's Rebellion and the Ratification of the Federal Constitution in Massachusetts," in Richard R. Beeman, Stephen Botein, and Edward C. Carter, eds., *Beyond Confederation: Origins of the Constitution and American National Identity* (1987), David P. Szatmary, *Shays' Rebellion: The Making of an Agrarian Insurrection* (1980), Rakove, *The Beginnings of National Politics*, G. S. Rowe, *Thomas McKean: The Shaping of an American Republicanism* (1978), Peter S. Onuf, *Statehood and Union: A History of the Northwest Ordinance* (1987) and *The Origins of the Federal Republic: Jurisdictional Controversies in the United States, 1775–1787* (1983), R. L. Cayton, *The Frontier Republic: Ideology and Politics in The Ohio Country, 1780–1825* (1986), and Bernard Bailyn, "Fulfillment: A Commentary on the Constitution," *The Ideological Origins of the American Revolution*, enlarged edition (1992).

The most recent scholarship on Shays's Rebellion and the Constitution is collected in Robert A. Gross, ed., *In Debt to Shays: The Bicentennial of an Agrarian Revolt.* Thomas E. Buckley, *Church and State in Revolutionary Virginia, 1776–1787* (1977), William Lee Miller, *The First Liberty: Religion and the American Republic* (1986), and Daniel L. Dreisbach, "A New Perspective on Jefferson's Views on Church-State Relations: The Virginia Statute for Establishing Religious Freedom in its Legislative Context," *American Journal of Legal History* (1991) are the basic works on Madison's defeat of religious assessment and the enactment of Jefferson's Statute of Religious Freedom.

The best recent works on the Constitution are Beeman, Botein, and Carter, eds., *Beyond Confederation* and the July 1987 *William and Mary Quarterly*, a special issue on the Constitution. Donald S. Lutz, *The Origins of American Constitutionalism* (1988) is an excellent overview. On Madison's role in the first weeks of the Convention, see Jack N. Rakove, "The Great Compromise: Ideas, Interests, and the

Politics of Constitution Making," *William and Mary Quarterly* (1987) and Rossiter, *1787: The Grand Convention*. On Dickinson's role, see Rakove, "The Great Compromise..." and James H. Hutson, "John Dickinson at the Federal Constitutional Convention," *William and Mary Quarterly* (1983). On Madison's shift from critic to champion of the Great Compromise, see Lance Banning, "The Practicable Sphere of a Republic: James Madison, the Constitutional Convention, and the Emergence of Revolutionary Federalism," in Beeman, Botein, and Carter, eds., *Beyond Confederation*. On the paradoxical internal strategy of the drafters of the Constitution, see Charles F. Hobson, "The Negative on State Laws: James Madison and the Crisis of Republican Government," *William and Mary Quarterly* (1979), Paul Finkelman, "Slavery and the Constitutional Convention: Making a Covenant with Death," in Beeman, Botein, and Carter, eds., *Beyond Confederation*, and Ralph Ketcham, *Presidents above Party: The First American Presidency, 1789–1829* (1984), especially chapter 10.

Michael Lienesch, *New Order of the Ages: Time, the Constitution, and the Making of Modern American Political Thought* (1988) examines the framers' worries about time and contingency—how to seize the moment when the moment is fleeting. On the liberal individualism of the Constitution, see John P. Diggins, *The Lost Soul of American Politics: Virtue, Self-Interest, and the Foundations of Liberalism* (1984) and J. R. Pole, "The Individualist Foundations of American Constitutionalism," in Herman Belz, Ronald Hoffman, and Peter J. Albert, eds., *To Form a More Perfect Union: The Critical Ideas of the Constitution* (1992).

On the *Federalist Papers*, see Colbourn, ed., *The Spur of Fame*, Daniel W. Howe, "The Political Psychology of *The Federalist*," *William and Mary Quarterly* (1987), and David F. Epstein, *The Political Theory of the Federalist* (1984). Further evidence of the utility of Scottish moral philosophy appears in Garry Wills, "James Wilson's New Meaning for Sovereignty," in Terrence Bell and J. G. A. Pocock, eds., *Conceptual Change and the Constitution* (1988) and Shannon C. Stimson, "A Jury of the Country': Common Sense Philosophy and the Jurisprudence of James Wilson," in Richard B. Sher and Jeffrey R. Smitten, eds., *Scotland and America in the Age of the Enlightenment*. J. G. A. Pocock, "Cambridge Paradigms and Scotch Philosophers: A Study of the Relations between the Civic Humanist and the Jurisprudential Interpretation of Eighteenth-Century Social Thought," in Istvan Hont and Michael Ignatieff, eds., *Wealth and Virtue: The Shaping of Political Economy in the Scottish Enlightenment* (1984) casts doubt on the republican credentials of the Scottish moral philosophers.

On the role of republicanism in the politics of the 1790s, see Joyce Appleby, *Capitalism and a New Social Order: The Republican Vision of the 1790s* (1984), McDonald, *The Presidency of George Washington*, Ralph Adams Brown, *The Presidency of John Adams* (1975), James M. Banner, *To the Hartford Convention: The Federalists and the Origins of Party Government in Massachusetts, 1789–1815* (1970), and Thomas P. Slaughter, *The Whiskey Rebellion: Frontier Epilogue to the American Revolution* (1986), and two classic studies of the respective tendencies in American republicanism: Lance Banning, *The Jeffersonian Persuasion: Evolution of a Party Ideology* and Gerald Stourzh, *Alexander Hamilton and the Idea of Republican Government* (1970). John R. Howe, *Liberty and Property: Political Economy and Policymaking in the New Nation, 1789–1812* (1987) is a searching critique of Hamilton's statecraft. Merrill D. Peterson, *Thomas Jefferson and the New Nation* (1970) discusses the ideas in documents like his first inaugural address in 1801.

Afterword

For the widening of differences over ideology among historians, see Greene's articles, "Political Mimesis: A Reconsideration of the British Colonies in the Eighteenth Century," *American Historical Review* (1969) and "The Social Origins of the American Revolution: An Evaluation and an Interpretation," *Political Science Quarterly* (1973). Bernard Bailyn, "The Central Themes of the American Revolution: An Interpretation," in Stephen G. Kurtz and James H. Hutson, eds., *Essays on the American Revolution* (1973), expresses reservations concerning a republican interpretation of the early national period, and Bailyn's "Fulfillment: A Commentary on the Constitution" explores the way instrumental ideology supplanted moral ideology in 1787–1788. John P. Diggins, *The Lost Soul of American Politics* is a brilliant wide-ranging, polemical critique of the republican interpretation. In contrast, see J. G. A. Pocock, "States, Republics, and Empires: The American Founding in Early Modern Perspective," Ball and Pocock, eds., *Conceptual Change and the Constitution* (1988).

John M. Murrin, "Fundamental Values, the Founding Fathers, and the Constitution," in Belz, Hoffman, and Albert, eds., *To Form a More Perfect Union* locates common ground in this debate, as does J. Thomas Wren, "The Ideology of Court and Country in the Virginia Ratifying Convention of 1788," *Virginia Magazine of History and Biography* (1985). Banning, "Jeffersonian Ideology Revisited: Liberal and Classical Ideas in the Early American Republic," Appleby, "Republicanism in Old and New Contexts," in *Liberalism and Republicanism in Historical Imagination*, restate their positions and narrow somewhat their differences. Kloppenberg, "The Virtues of Liberalism: Christianity, Republicanism, and Ethics in Early American Discourse," is a highly original fusion of insights from the republican and liberal interpretations. Wood upholds the republican ideology in "Conspiracy and the Paranoid Style: Causality and Deceit in the Eighteenth Century," *William and Mary Quarterly* (1982) by means of an elaborate discussion of epistemology—the nature of knowledge in early modern culture. The most recent discussion of the issue is Milton M. Klein, Richard D. Brown, and John B. Hench, eds., *The Republican Synthesis Revisited* (1992).

The splintering of republicanism in the early nineteenth century can be traced in Norman K. Risjord, *The Old Republicans: Southern Conservatives in the Age of Jefferson* (1965), Roger H. Brown, *The Republic in Peril: 1812* (1964), and Drew R. McCoy, *The Last of the Fathers: James Madison and the Republican Legacy* (1989).

On the appropriation of republicanism in popular politics, see Eric Foner, *Free Labor, Free Soil, Free Men: The Ideology of the Republican Party before the Civil War* (1970), Wilentz, *Democratic Chants*, John L. Brooke, *The Heart of the Commonwealth: Society and Political Culture in Worcester County Massachusetts, 1713–1861* (1989), Hatch, *Democratization of American Christianity*, and the essays by Daniel Walker Howe and Bertram Wyatt-Brown in Mark A. Noll, ed., *Religion and American Politics: From the Colonial Period to the 1980s* (1990).

The republican shaping of the law is treated in Richard A. Brisbin, "John Marshall and the Nature of the Law in the Early Republic," *Virginia Magazine of History and Biography* (1990), Morton J. Horwitz, *The Transformation of American Law, 1780–1860* (1977), James Henretta, "The Slow Triumph of Liberal Individualism: Law and Politics in New York, 1780–1860," in Richard O. Curry and Larry B.

Goodheart, eds., *American Chameleon: Individualism in Trans-National Context* (1991), and R. Kent Newmyer, *Supreme Court Justice Joseph Story: Statesman of the Old Republic* (1985).

Michael Johnson, *Toward a Patriarchal Republic: The Secession of Georgia* (1977) explores proslavery republicanism. On Calhoun as a republican theorist, see J. William Harris, "Last of the Classical Republicans: An Interpretation of John C. Calhoun," *Civil War History* (1984) and Calhoon, *Evangelicals and Conservatives in the Early South.* Garry Wills, *Lincoln at Gettysburg* (1992) complements the same author's *Cincinnatus.* Richard C. Sinopoli, *The Foundations of American Citizenship* argues that republicanism fortified the bedrock liberalism of the founders and applies that analysis to the contemporary crisis of civic consciousness in American life. Stanley Elkins and Eric McKitrick, *The Age of Federalism* (1993) is a magisterial work on the values of the Founding Fathers.

Index

Dominion and Liberty: Ideology in the Anglo-American World, 1660–1801
Copyeditor, Andrew J. Davidson
Production editor, Lucy Herz
Typesetter, Point West, Inc.
Printer, McNaughton & Gunn, Inc.
Book designer, Roger Eggers

About the Author: Robert M. Calhoon is Professor of History at the University of North Carolina at Greensboro. Professor Calhoon's other books include *The Loyalist Perception and Other Essays; Evangelicals and Conservatives in the Early South; The Loyalists in Revolutionary America, 1760–1781;* and *Revolutionary America,* for which he won the William R. Davie Award for the best book written in North Carolina on the Revolution in 1976.